The

Guerrilla

Sniper

Tactics

Handbook

Copyright© 2016 by Roy A Woodall, Jr.

All rights reserved, including the right to reproduce this book or the portions thereof in any form whatsoever.

ISBN-13: 978-1534991606

ISBN-10: 1534991603

The Guerrilla Sniper Tactics Handbook

By Roy A Woodall Jr

Also by the author

The Art of Warrior Leadership

The Scout Sniper Tactics Handbook

Military and Police Tactics

The Combat Leaders Training Handbook

From A to Zen: Seven Days to Inner Peace and Calm

When Good Times Go Bad

The United Nations Tactical Handbook

Dedication

To all the free people of the world I hope you never need this book.

To those living under the boot of tyranny…start reading.

Give me liberty or give me death

Patrick Henry

Introduction 1

1. The Guerrilla Sniper 7

2. Strategic Principles of Guerrilla Sniper Operations 21

3. Purpose, Motivation, and Combat Mindset 31

4. The Principles of Small Group Leadership 39

5. Raids and Ambushes 49

6. Sniper Tactics and Observation Techniques 65

7. Understanding Wind and Unknown Ranges 87

8. Sniper Tactics Techniques Procedures 95

9. Survival Evasion and Recovery 105

10. Handgun Selection for the Sniper 117

11. Global Positioning Systems 123

12. Guerrilla Sniper Training 141

13. Conducting Guerrilla Sniper Operations 149

14. Intelligence Gathering for Future Operations 159

15. Mission Planning and Preparation 165

16. Fundamentals of Man Tracking 173

About the Author 209

The Guerrilla Sniper Tactics Handbook

Introduction

If I were to wake up one morning and look around to see that I was living in enemy occupied territory as a subject of some tyrannical government, it would mean that my government had been overrun and the military had been defeated. I, like many others, would want to evade the enemy and fight to the bitter end. Knowledge, courage, and hidden weapons are great but how can one person have a reasonable expectation of winning against a professional army. Going head to head with the new government's forces is paramount to suicide so the key to success is in not fighting them directly. History has shown that freedom loving individuals can join together to wear down and defeat a tyrannical government by engaging in a political war using guerrilla tactics.

The purpose of this book is strictly educational; knowledge is power. While it is true that citizens of any country can lose their freedoms overnight from foreign invaders, they can also lose those same freedoms slowly over time through apathy. Whenever we see these warning signs of tyranny creeping in we should fight back using whatever legal peaceful means that are available. Politicians want to keep their jobs and will support the majority way of thinking. If enough freedom loving people stick together, speak out, and stay involved in

[handwritten: majority = mob unless educated. Distinguish yourself from the majority through education.]

> The integrity of that process must be
> first order of business
> + Democratic via thuggery stole the 2020 Presidential election
>
> State Police should ensure access to poll watchers

The Guerrilla Sniper Tactics Handbook

the political process by voting we will not lose anything. The ability to resist an all powerful evil government is the first step toward preventing an all powerful evil government. The ancient Greek philosophy of "Si vis pacam, para bellum" (if you want peace prepare for war) is truer now than ever. Preparing for an armed resistance prevents one. So it is the obligation of every freedom loving person to educate themselves, arm themselves, and keep a skeptical eye on our elected leaders.

The new government's forces will show no mercy to the resistance fighter so becoming a guerrilla is no small act of patriotism. Guerrillas will be branded as insurgents, terrorists, and traitors. They will be hunted down, put on trial, and quickly executed. History has been kind to the countless citizens turned soldiers a long time ago who took up arms against King George III's soldiers breaking the colonial bond and making the way for the United States of America. History has countless examples of how patriots working in secret have been able to wage war against kings, dictators, and tyrannical governments. The line between the criminal and the patriot can be pretty blurry especially when the government controls the information. Whether these people are truly patriots or criminals depends who your point of view and who you ask. Never forget that to the government that they resist they are criminals. It seems to me that if you win you get to call yourself whatever you want.

Values are a major part of everyone's lives and are big factor in someone's willingness to kill. Whether you are a Christian, Muslim, Buddhist, or Atheist, you have a belief system that you live by. I was in Afghanistan in 2013 interviewing military aged males to determine if they were sympathetic to the Taliban and noticed that every single male I interviewed was blatantly lying to me about everything. I asked my interpreter, who was Muslim "why are they lying so much if it is against their religion?" His answer to me was "it was not wrong to lie to an infidel". My thought then and now is that Muslims have a distinct religious advantage over Christians because they are instructed from birth that they can do whatever they want to infidels. Christian values like to turn the other cheek, do not kill, do not lie, and do not steal are always going to be in conflict with the Guerrilla Sniper. I am not a religious person and my values are best represented by the Italian philosopher Niccola Machiavelli which is why several of his quotes are in this book. I live my life by my own sense of right and wrong and refuse to be influenced by others who report to be speaking for god, the government, or whoever. My power and my strength come from inside me and I will forgive who I choose to forgive and I will kill who I choose to kill.

Yes, be willing but let God guide your conscience.

The guerrilla sniper handbook is a book of tactics, concepts, and ideas. This handbook purposely does not contain long lists of firearms, optics, and gear. Anyone who spends enough time behind a precision rifle will figure out what equipment they prefer anyway. This handbook is intended to educate the reader on the tactics, techniques, and procedures of guerrilla sniping knowing that any good scrounger can cobble together an accurate scoped rifle, camouflage clothing, and all the tactical gear necessary to carry out successful guerrilla operations.

How to Maximize Your Training

I have been fortunate to be able to participate in a lot of training courses as a soldier and police officer over the last 20 years as both the student and the instructor. It took me a while to come to the conclusion that the biggest factor in my enjoying a course and learning something meaningful was not the curriculum, the topic, or the instructor but it was my attitude. Realizing that my attitude was so critical I developed a training strategy that I now implement prior to and during every class. This strategy has really allowed me to maximize my learning and get the most for my time and money.

As a student it's important to support the instructor so the best way we can do this is by showing up well rested and with a positive attitude. Getting adequate sleep and abstaining from alcohol the night before training goes a long way towards showing up ready to learn. When I am attending a firearms training class that is physically demanding I try to get up early and hit the gym for a light workout for the purpose of getting warmed up to reduce the chance of injury. Another tip I learned was getting all my required equipment organized and stowed a few days prior to the course so I didn't forget something. Nothing ruins a day at the range like forgetting critical equipment. Before I attend any training I also set a goal of what I want to learn while I am there. It seems for me that going in with a goal completely changes my expectations and makes the experience much more enjoyable. Once I get to training I really try to listen and keep my talking to a minimum. It's best to have an open mind when it comes to new information and not to form opinions too early. In some cases it may take a few days or weeks to truly understand something so don't be in a hurry to love or hate something. One of the biggest roadblocks to learning is ego. Nobody wants to be seen not knowing something so we resist doing new things outside our comfort zones especially when others are watching. It's ironic that we spend time and money to take a training class and spend most of that time trying to show the instructor and fellow students how much we already know.

The bottom line is to get the most of any training experience, show up rested, with the right attitude, have goals, and put the ego aside. These seemingly simple ideas took me years to realize but once I implemented them my training got better, I learned more, and I felt like my time and money were better spent

Chapter 1

The Guerrilla Sniper

There comes a time when diplomacy fails, when all discussion is fruitless.

You will then face me under a different and final circumstance.

Col. Michael Hoare

The Guerrilla Sniper

He walks to the edge of town careful to see if he is being followed, he isn't. He waits there for a while finally concealing himself behind the brush just watching the road. He turns into the forest and begins to walk careful that he is not being followed or watched. [1 hide entry/exit pt] His footsteps are slow and deliberate while his head moves around looking and seeing everything. With every step civilization slips away and the hunter of men returns. When he locates the bag he hid there [2 a good place for traps] just days ago, he carefully looks it over, confident it has not been tampered with, and he retrieves it. He them moves deeper into the forest. He opens the bag and removed the contents. Inside the bag are all the tools of the sniper, a folding stock sniper rifle, a well crafted ghillie suit, boots, and a small chest rig containing ammo, water, survival kit, and maps. He quickly removes all of his city clothes folding them neatly, placing them in the bag. Now dressed as the sniper he applies camouflage paste to his hands and face. Fully concealed he moves slowly to the ridge overlooking the main road to town. The road is now being used by the new government's forces as a main supply route. With his map he locates his position and determines the distance to the bend in the road is 600 [3] yards to the center; an easy shot.

1. A good point to ditch your shoes + put on moccasins
3. range finder. No map recon in town, hide the map its evidence.

A few hours later he sees the vehicles before he hears them. The lead vehicle in the convoy is the local commander of the new government's forces. As they approached the turn in the road the sniper takes careful aim and shoots the driver of the unarmored vehicle through the front windshield. He watches as the vehicle swerves suddenly hitting a nearby tree and blocking the narrow road. The remaining trucks behind the commander's vehicle are forced to stop. He watches as the many soldiers riding inside the convoy get out wildly pointing their rifles towards the trees trying desperately to locate their attacker. The soldiers are well organized ready to defend themselves against a conventional attack but the lone sniper continually eludes and frustrates them. The sniper calmly waits for the commander who takes a while to get out of his vehicle; he looks to have been injured in the accident. As the commander emerges he starts yelling and waving his arms to rally his troops to attack. The sniper places the rifle's cross hairs on the center of the commander's chest. With his second and final shot the commander is dead; permanently removed from the battlefield. The sniper then moves slowly back and away from his hide only breaking into a run after hearing the now leaderless troops firing wildly into the forest at shapes and shadows. He simply melts back into the forest finding a new place to conceal his deadly tools. He changes back into his civilian clothes, carefully cleaning his hands and face removing all traces of the camouflage paste. With his new hiding place secure, the sniper slowly walks out of the forest and blends back into the local population without giving any suspicion of his well planned and executed ambush. He returns to his unimportant job where he looks, listens, and plans for the next attack. Someday he thinks "I will break the will of these foreign invaders".

What is a "guerrilla" and what does it mean?

The word guerrilla comes from the Spanish language literally translating to "little war". The term came into use in the 18th century during the Peninsular War when the Spanish people rose up against the highly superior Napoleonic troops using unconventional military tactics. The term is now meant to describe a strategy as well as an individual or groups of combatants fighting against a conventional army.

Sniper as a tactic

There are soldiers and police officers who have the job description of sniper. These individuals are selected, school trained, and then deploy to support conventional forces providing precision rifle fire and to gather intelligence for their leadership. Using sniper tactics means ambushing someone from a long distance, using a concealed/camouflaged position, and then using fire discipline to remain undetected. For the sake of this manual, when we discuss the guerrilla sniper, it is referring to a guerrilla, revolutionary, or partisan using sniper tactics to bring about the defeat of a tyrannical government.

or insurgent supporting displaced or establishment supporter - militia, or posse

What is precision rifle and how accurate does it need to be?

The sniper's rifle has to be durable and accurate. How accurate is a matter of discussion but generally speaking it should be capable of maintaining a consistent zero and be able to shoots groups no bigger than 12 inches at 600 yards. The smaller the groups size the better because it will allow the sniper to engage smaller targets like a partially exposed man's head. The snipers rifle should be equipped with a good quality scope. How powerful the scope is another debated topic but a good rule of thumb is 1 power per 100 meters. Since

- M14A1 or FAL - maybe Remington 700 7mm Mag - 270-280. 6.5

6X -

the sniper wants to engage targets from a safe distance like 600 yards for a rural setting so a six power scope would be sufficient but a ten power would be better. Guerrilla snipers engaged in urban combat are better served with a variable powered scope and in my experience 3.5 - 10 power is ideal. Bottom line is the better the rifle the farther the sniper can shoot and shooting too close will likely get the sniper detected and destroyed.

There is no better tool for the guerrilla than a precision rifle

When we talk about getting the "most bang for the buck" the guerrilla sniper is the perfect example. With some training, minimal equipment, and minimal logistical support a single rifleman/sharpshooter can grind a conventional army to a halt. When you add a scope to an already accurate rifle and then put that rifle into the hands of a marksman using sniper tactics he becomes a force multiplier. With the scoped precision rifle a moderately trained guerrilla sniper can easily engage man sized targets out to 600 yards while a highly trained guerrilla sniper may be able to make hits out to 1000 yards. The precision rifle has a distinct ballistic advantage over assault rifles and by understanding this and exploiting this is the key to success. The guerrilla sniper who knows the area, is comfortable living off the land, and has the strategic mind of a stone cold killer is the worst nightmare of military commander who is trying to occupy territory and minimize his own soldier's casualties.

How does guerrilla sniper differ from a conventional army or police sniper?

- Psychological effect
- As a propaganda tool
- Targets not limited to leadership and key personnel
- More effective as a lone wolf and not part of a group
- Motivated by ideology, self trained, and self selected. Not a school trained sniper
- The guerrilla sniper gathers his own intelligence and selects his own targets
- Uses knowledge of the terrain and relies on support from the locals
- Not limited by the rules of war, commanders intent, or conventional tactics

Psychological effect

Snipers can be used as psychological tool by having an overwhelming demoralizing effect on the new government's forces because they cannot fight an enemy they cannot find. Soldiers are naturally fearful of going on patrol but imagine them being fearful of being shot when waiting in line for food or being shot while walking to the latrine or shower. When you give them no place to feel safe it will have a corrosive effect on moral and the new government's forces will see their leadership as ineffective.

As a propaganda tool

The Sniper can provoke an overreaction of the new government's forces to attack unarmed civilians. The end result would be used for propaganda purposes to influence the media and draw international attention. The provocation starts when the sniper positions himself on the far side of a group of civilians, positioning the civilians in between himself and the new government's forces. The sniper then engages the new government's force in an attempt to provoke and draw return gun fire putting the civilians at risk. This technique was used in Iraq against US forces and drew international attention just like it was intended.

There have been instances where the crowd has deceased children who have died from disease, concealed until after the attack and then pass the dead children off as victims of the attack. These propaganda tools are extremely effective and rely heavily on deception. If coordinated in advance like the above example, civilian casualties can easily be staged or exaggerated. The important part of using propaganda is the perception not the reality.

Targets are not limited to leadership and key personnel

Professional snipers supporting tactical teams and tactical operations are only going to engage equipment and individuals that support the operation and don't violate the commander's rules. The guerrilla sniper on the other hand is free to engage and kill seemingly unimportant soldiers because that supports the psychological effect of making every soldier feel unsafe. A good tactic is to engage the new government's troops at their base so they will organize a counter attack. The sniper then leaves the area only to return later and engages them again. The purpose of the tactic is to cause frustration and fatigue.

Is it better to be a lone wolf or part of a cell?

Security is always going to be the biggest concern for the Guerrilla Sniper. The more skilled the sniper is the more resources will be allocated by the government to detect, locate, and kill him. While the best security is to operate as a lone wolf, the guerrilla sniper may choose to affiliate with a terrorist cell to benefit from their resources. By affiliating with the cell the guerrilla sniper can gain access to additional intelligence, money, and equipment. Guerrilla cells are commonly infiltrated by double agents, spies, and will be a constant target of government forces. So whether it is best to be a lone wolf or not depends on the situation. A cell that is found to be reckless, has poor security, and lacks good leadership is probably best avoided. My instincts lean heavily toward the lone wolf guerrilla sniper. I believe that the solo operator has the best likelihood of success and will survive longer than those affiliated with cells.

Motivated by ideology, self trained, and self selected. Not a school trained sniper

Military and police snipers are highly trained and carefully selected for their patience, maturity, intelligence and tactical shooting ability. Once they are selected they are sent to formal sniper schools where they are instructed in the tactics, techniques, and procedures (TTPs) of sniping. While at school they are given ample time to develop and practice these TTPs. While the guerrilla sniper may have similar skills and abilities, he does not wait to be selected, trained, and equipped. The guerrilla sniper chooses to be a sniper, locates the needed equipment, and self trains often while conducting sniper missions. The guerrilla sniper is not motivated by a desire for shooting but instead uses shooting to bring about a change in the government by attempting to overthrow and undermine a totalitarian system. Many of these self appointed snipers will be killed right away but a small few will survive and become very skilled at hunting and killing.

The guerrilla sniper gathers his own intelligence and selects his own targets

It is the responsibility of the conventional military and police snipers commanders to provide material support, up to date intelligence, and predetermined targets to the snipers assigned to their command. The guerrilla sniper has none of these luxuries, therefore he must gather his own intelligence and select his own targets. Intelligence can be gathered by simply watching the new government's forces to determine their routine and structure. Also the local populace can be an invaluable source of intelligence. Target selection may be something as simple as "drive down to the nearby army base and find someone to shoot at" or something more complex like a high value dignitary. However the guerrilla chooses his target is entirely dependent on the situation. A strategic approach is often the prudent choice, but sometimes luck does favor bold impulsive choices. One simple but highly effective target opportunity is to paint some anti government slogan on a wall and then wait to see who shows up to remove it.

Uses knowledge of the terrain and relies on support from the locals

The guerrilla sniper has a real advantage of fighting in his homeland. He knows the language, the culture, and the people. He may be operating miles away from where he was born and raised. The most effective guerrilla knows every hollow tree, every ditch, and cave that can be used to hide food, water, ammo, and sniper gear. The guerrilla sniper does not have to rely on night vision goggles for navigation because he can walk through the area blind folded and have a pretty good chance of not getting lost. He uses his personal knowledge to outfox his enemy and predict their movements. The guerrilla sniper also relies on the support of the local populace who must remain sympathetic, providing him with money, information, shelter, food, and water. Locals can serve as lookouts in urban combat and provide up to date target information by relaying to the sniper with cell phones. Guerrillas who threaten, harass, and exploit the locals run the risk of them aligning with the new government's forces. It is important to portray the new government's forces as foreign invaders and the guerrillas as fighting for the freedom of everyone. <u>The locals must not lose hope or believe that victory is unobtainable</u>. The relationship between the guerrilla and the local population needs to be maintained.

Not limited by the rules of war, commanders intent, or conventional tactics

The guerrilla sniper is free to roam the battlefield seeking out opportunities to engage the new government's forces without the same responsibilities as conventional forces. He is free of the rules of war, he can engage non combatants at will, and has no commanders to second guess his decisions. The guerrilla sniper only has to focus on the life and death of the situation.

This page intentionally left blank

Chapter 2

Strategic Principles of Conducting Guerrilla Sniper Operations

Every normal man must be tempted at times to spit upon his hands, hoist the black flag, and begin slitting throats.

H.L. Mencken

Strategic Principles of Conducting Guerrilla Sniper Operations

Guerrilla warfare has a long and fascinating history going back thousands of years beginning with what many think are the writings of Sun Tzu. Just in the last 70 years we have some more recent examples that are worth our study. Whether we consider these guerrillas to be heroes or criminals matters little because what we are interested in is the tactics they used and whether those tactics were effective for their particular situation.

- Vietnam 1945 - 1975 The Vietcong were able to shatter western dominance by giving a humiliating defeat to France in the battle of Dien Bien Phu and later forced the United States to leave their county without defeating communism. Despite having huge financial support, a better military, and the support from numerous other countries they could not defeat the Vietcong.
- Cuba 1955 - 1959 The July 26 Movement. Fidel Castro, Che Guevara, and their group of 82 were able to overthrow the rule of Fulgencio Batista and defeat his army of more than 20,000 soldiers.
- Afghanistan 1979 - 1989 The Mujahideen kept the Soviet Union from fully occupying the mountainous country for more than a decade because

of their guerrilla tactics and support from the United States, Pakistan, and Saudi Arabia. The Soviet Union ultimately left the county despite having tanks, helicopters, and a far superior army.

There is no doubt that groups can accomplish more than individuals, but don't underestimate the ability of a motivated, self sufficient, and tactical minded person working alone. The independent guerrilla sniper can conduct successful tactical operations by combining a simple plan with an unwavering commitment to the objective. The lone wolf or solo military operator requires less logistical support making them easier to fund and harder to detect. A successful guerrilla sniper combines the characteristics, skills, and mindset of the ultra light backpacker, mountain man, and commando. There are military skills that give someone lethal capability but understanding strategic principles can give the guerrilla sniper "the big picture" needed to define their capability and lay a foundation for successful tactical operations. The most important lesson anyone can get from reading this book it to develop a strategic mindset.

What type of military operations can a single guerrilla sniper conduct?

- Reconnaissance
- Raids
- Ambush
- Sabotage
- Assassination

Ten strategic principles for successful guerrilla sniper operations

1. **Commitment**

The guerrilla must be committed to the cause of overthrowing the tyrannical government. It takes charismatic leaders to motivate and inspire the guerrilla fighters to their cause. This commitment should be the driving force behind every tactical operation. Charismatic caring leaders need to portray a positive vision of what freedom looks like. Human beings can endure severe hardship if given a sufficient reason for their sacrifice.

2. Work within your limits

Operations should be planned around "the most bang for the buck principle" with each operation supporting the strategic goal of victory. By keeping the operations as short as possible, the need for water, food and sleep can be minimized, therefore reducing material support needed for the mission. If an operation can't be completed within a few hours, its objectives should be broken up into smaller missions. The best results will come from being realistic and strategic.

3. Do not be limited by your knowledge

If you are a veteran of the U.S. Army Infantry you have been trained extensively on the commander's intent, mission planning, 5 paragraph operations order, troop leading procedures, rules of engagement, escalation of force, and countless other principles of modern warfare. These principles are necessary when working with conventional troops but these ideas can be unnecessary and tedious when planning independent guerrilla operations. It may be comforting to stay with what we know but realize how that may stifle creativity. Unconventional warfare relies on unconventional tactics and thinking. Also consider that most sniper training consists of lessons learned from previous conflicts. While these lessons learned are valuable training tools they may or may not be applicable to the current situation. When it comes to guerrilla warfare, using common sense, keeping things simple, and being based in reality is the key to success.

4. Simplicity

Choose simple direct plans that have the highest likelihood of success. Overly complicated plans often fail because the tactical operation loses momentum. Simple plans are also easy to remember and harder to detect.

5. Tactical flexibility

The guerrilla sniper has some advantages and disadvantages when compared to the conventional sniper. The major advantages are that the guerrilla is not limited in tactics, rules or war, or leadership restrictions. The disadvantages are that the guerrilla sniper may have little or no medical support, access to up to date intelligence, or formal training. The guerrilla sniper has the ability to define the battle by choosing when to attack and using the tactics that best fit the circumstance therefore maximizing the advantages and minimizing the disadvantages. Forcing the enemy to fight when they are not ready is a real advantage. The new government's forces cannot fight the guerrilla sniper when they cannot find the guerrilla sniper.

6. Always have a tangible objective

Guerrilla warfare is a political war. Every battle or attack must be directed towards a precisely defined and clearly described tangible objective that supports the overall political goals. The tangible objective must be the "master" or "controlling" principle because it is the basis from which all plans are formed. Freedom, hope, and change are not tangible objectives; they are inspirational ideas. Resources are limited to the guerrilla and must not be squandered. Always have an answer to the question; what are we trying to accomplish?

7. Defensive operations should be avoided

Do not make a base camp. Do not fill one sandbag. A guerrilla sniper is a nomad. He must pop up where he is least expected and never remain in one position too long. Survival relies on mobility, stealth, and deception. The guerrilla sniper must keep the enemy confused about his exact location or give the new government's forces the impression of a larger attacking force. The tactic of those hunting the sniper will be that of "find, fix, and finish" so if he gets detected his position will get fixed and he will be captured or killed.

8. Stealth

The new government's forces will use every available resource to detect and destroy the guerrilla sniper. He must be like a ghost. Stealth needs to be an essential aspect of all of the snipers planning and operations. Even the snipers existence should be a closely guarded secret. The guerrilla sniper will have the initial advantage but as the new government's forces get better at searching and hunting the later advantage will be theirs. Think of the identity of the guerrilla sniper as a puzzle. The longer he operates the more pieces of the puzzle will be exposed. The initial success before the enemy has a chance to get organized may be a false impression of their capability. Also the new government's forces commander may request additional assets to deal with a particularly effective sniper.

9. Speed, surprise, and violence of action

Speed is essential to tactical operations because once the attack is discovered the new government's forces will defend against the attack. Surprise is achieved by "striking" at an unanticipated time or place or in an unexpected manner. Violence is about hitting with enough force to destroy or harass the target. The counter tactic to speed, surprise, and violence of action is deter, detect, delay, and destroy. The first tactic employed in the defense against the attackers is to slow down the attacking force therefore robbing them of speed and also surprise.

10. Security

Security is essential to the mission success. Plans known are plans defeated. Security enhances freedom of action by reducing friendly vulnerability to hostile acts, influence or surprise. One of the biggest threats to the guerrilla will be enemy spies attempting to locate the members of the guerrilla force to arrest them, interrogate them, and turn them into double agents. Information is power and it must be protected.

This page is intentionally left blank

Chapter 3

Purpose, Motivation, and Combat Mindset

Leaders and warriors are not born, they are made.

Purpose, Motivation, and Combat Mindset

Purpose

A sniper is a critical member of a tactical team and the amount of skill and knowledge required to be a modern sniper is staggering. Whether the sniper is a member of a SWAT team or a soldier in a war zone, a sniper must master marksmanship, maintain a heightened level of fitness, and learn to think like those they hunt. The purpose of this manual is to document the tips, tricks, and lessons of sniper tactics that take years of blood, sweat, and tears to perfect. By documenting this information is gives the working sniper a handbook containing information to survive in combat and a reference to teach the next generation of shooter the tactics, techniques, and procedures of the sniper profession.

Motivation

I have always thought and stated that a sniper should be the best member of any tactical team. Often it's been asked by both new and old shooters alike what characteristics make the best snipers. Here is a list of traits that have been a guide to me and fellow warriors whom I have served.

- The ability to function forward in extreme circumstances

- Knowledge: both technical and tactical
- Positive Attitude
- Proper Fitness level
- Ability to function in and add value to a team
- The desire to learn and improve
- The willingness to do what most are too lazy to do
- Sound tactical judgment under stressful condition

Combat Mindset

Having been in combat and under fire I can say that establishing and maintaining combat mindset is essential to the survival of the mind and body when you are exposed to the toxic and corrosive environment of war. First it is important to prepare our minds for killing and develop a hunger for combat. If and when we become like the hunter looking for opportunities to fight then we immunize ourselves to the sometimes crippling effects of post traumatic stress. A warrior who is trained in the art of combat should be the one inflicting post traumatic stress disorders on others and not falling prey to its effects. Our country has been at war for a long time and it will likely get harder before there is peace. Being a warrior is an honorable profession and every warrior owes it to those they serve to be a subject matter expert in their profession. It is warriors that hold our society together and make the difference between order and chaos.

Psychological and physical responses to combat may include:

- Tunnel vision
- Auditory exclusion
- Fine motor skill degradation
- Fight or flight response

Remember: The closer we can get to the stresses of combat in training without compromising safety the more we can accurately measure performance and increase the likelihood of success in real combat.

Security Mindset and Warrior Thinking

(White) Unaware of surroundings

(Orange) Aware, tactical plan with constant what/ if thinking

(Red) Tactical plan in action adapt, kill, or be killed mentality (hunter)

(Black) Panic mode, tactical plan not initiated or failed, gave up (prey)

Color Codes of Situational Awareness

Part of developing a survival mindset is being aware of your situation. The military developed a set of color codes which Col. Jeff Cooper adapted for personal street survival.

Condition White

An individual in Condition White chooses to be totally unaware that the world is an unpredictable place and that full of life threatening or life changing events. In a make believe polite society where people only harm others by accident then living in condition white might be acceptable but in the real world where manmade or natural threats are around every corner then condition white sets you up to be a victim. White is like the fluffy little lamb waiting to be dined on by the pack of wolves. Victims live in condition white.

Condition Orange

Condition Orange is the realization and acceptance that we live in a dangerous world. It means we are aware of the general threats while constantly searching for specific threats. Someone in condition Orange has a constant tactical plan and updates that plan with when new information is obtained. Remember, it is the preparation to survive threats that facilitates the survival of threats.

Condition Red

Condition Red is when you see something specific and life threatening. The tactical plan is implemented; it's go time. Condition red is combat. The more you train for combat the easier it is to recognize and survive.

Condition Black

You are considered to be in condition black when you are in panic mode and not moving forward/back or taking any action. Freezing up will only make you a victim. Conditions that create condition black are lack of fitness, lack of commitment, and condition White thinking. There is a connection between surprise and panic. Avoid surprise to avoid panic

Remember: Nobody sneaks up on a warrior.

This page intentionally left blank

Chapter 4

The Principles of Small Group Leadership:

Lead Follow or Get Out of The Way

Never was anything great achieved without danger

Niccolo Machiavelli

The Principles of Small Group Leadership:

Lead Follow or Get Out of The Way

Being the boss or being in charge means different things to different people. Just having an important title does not make someone a leader and that title alone will do little to attract the respect of a team. Every type A personality group I have worked with had a "show me what you can do, don't tell me" mindset. Being a leader of a small specialized tactical team requires more than just basic managerial skills it requires dedication, devotion, and a complete understanding of the mission. Small teams are like families which can be both good and bad because when you work closely with people you are exposed to their character, values, and choices. The most effective small group leaders are the ones that are respected by their subordinates because the team trusts their skills, judgment, and decisions.

In 2008 I attended a week long SWAT school called "Hell Week". I was already an established member of my city's SWAT team and I had attended all of the required training but I was hungry for more. I wanted more knowledge, more experience, and another "gut check". I found the training opportunity I was looking for in a neighboring jurisdiction's SWAT school. They used hell week as a selection for new their new SWAT officers and to provide new officers in the fundamentals of SWAT tactics and techniques. The course was intended to be intense with a high drop-out rate hence the name "Hell Week". I received permission from my department to attend as long it was at my own time and my own expense. The course was open to any police officer or sheriff deputy from a various organizations so the teams were made up of complete strangers. We were organized into multiple ten man teams. Each team competed against the other throughout the week in multiple challenges with the reward of bragging rights and a few extra moments of rest. By the end of the week my entire team was sleep deprived, bruised, but otherwise invincible. My team had bonded like a true family and as each challenge got more complex and more difficult we became more dedicated to each other and success. On the last day as part of the graduation requirement each team was required to run an obstacle course that was over a mile long with all sorts of barriers each built for the sole purpose of causing pain. As my team began the obstacle course one of our very first challenges was to get the entire team dressed in full tactical gear and weapons over a 15 foot smooth concrete wall. As we ran toward that wall my initial impression was that without a ladder or some sort of rope in place we were not getting over. As we reached the base of the wall we pushed the smallest team member to the top of the wall so he could pull the rest of us up. We sent the biggest guy next and so on until each and every one of use got up and over. Within a few short moments all ten of us were over and on the other side running onto the next challenge. It was when I saw my entire team on the ground running away from that obstacle I realized that a team of highly trained individuals that work together can accomplish almost anything. What I had falsely believed to be impossible was actually pretty easy. The motto of the organization, who hosted the training, is "Victoriam Obligamos" which translates to "committed to victory". Suffering through that course taught me many valuable lessons about small group leadership and about my own level of determination. I remind myself often to be committed to victory.

The principle of BE KNOW DO leadership

I learned the simple but profound principle of "**BE - KNOW - DO**" leadership from the United States Army early in my career. This concept is a standard in which I measure myself and strive for self improvement. It is about having rock solid job competence, personal courage, and core values that are essential when leading in the small group environment.

The **BE** principle is about your character as a leader and is foundational to your ability to lead. This is about the courage to do what it is right regardless of the circumstances or the consequences. As part of BE you should be aware of your personal core values as well as your organization's values. Be a man of action and stand by your character. Be value added every day. At a basic minimum the essential values every leader should hold are:

Loyalty – Be loyal to your country, your organization, and your people. Never forget the sacrifices that are made every day to maintain freedom. Leadership is a privilege.

Duty- Having a complete knowledge of the mission, how it's suppose to be accomplished even in the absence of further orders, and the internal obligation to make sure its completed.

Respect - Treat people how you want to be treated. Never forget the affect bad leaders had on you and how they compromised moral. Always praise in public discipline in private.

Selfless service - Never use your authority to elevate or enrich yourself. The mission, the team, and your subordinate come first. Take care of them and they will take care of you.

Honor - Knowing what right and wrong looks like and making sure our actions match our words. Honor in many ways sums up all of our values and puts them into action.

Integrity – As a leader you will have the discretion to make decisions that most people won't ever know about. A measure of Integrity is the choices and decisions that you make when nobody is looking.

Courage- There is two types of courage; Personal courage and moral courage. Personal courage is about being scared but choosing to go into harm's way trusting in your training and your subordinates. Moral courage is relying on your duty, honor, and integrity to make hard decisions and then standing by those decisions regardless of the consequences.

Interpersonal skill – Knowing how to read people is one of the most critical skills I learned as a police officer. A skilled caring leader knows his people. He knows what they can do and more importantly what they can't do. He realizes that the decisions he makes affects them on many levels and is not blind to their well being.

Conceptual skills – Everything and everyone are connected it is about seeing how that is important. Bad leaders often change rules without taking time to see the big picture and ultimately cause a ripple effect. Learn all the moving parts and see the big picture.

The **KNOW** principle is all about knowing your job and the job of everyone above and below you. Know the technical and know the tactical. There is no substitute for job knowledge and job skill. Remember that experience and competence is the eventual byproducts of training. New job assignments, promotions, and transfers equal lots and lots of training to get up to speed on the different skills. Don't be worried about being the "new guy". Know that mastering skills is essential to the success of your men and your mission. Don't fake it because people will know. Working closely with someone day after day will expose the cracks in your armor.

The last and final principle is the **DO** principle. As a leader you spent most of your time getting people to do what they don't want to do. The best leaders don't manage people instead they provide purpose, direction, and motivation. It comes down to bringing together everything you are, everything you believe, and everything you know. Simply put great leaders do the right thing at the right time for the right reasons.

Conclusion

When I was in Afghanistan I heard an analogy that I want to share. The analogy is that teams are like plywood. Think about how plywood is made up of small bits of wood that alone may not be able to accomplish much. You then take those small individual pieces and put them into a machine pressing them down. The next step is to add glue to the wood which holds it all together. What comes out of that machine is what we call plywood. Plywood is not always pretty and it may have a few imperfections here and there. You can make some pretty amazing things with plywood. Think of the organization as the machine and leaderships as the glue. People, like little bits of wood, with the right amount of glue and the right amount of pressure can do amazing things.

Throughout my law enforcement and military careers I have had the privilege and responsibility of being a member and a leader of several small tactical teams. It has been the most challenging and most rewarding part of my adult life. The lessons that I learned and the bonds that I have built will be with me always. To me honor, integrity, and courage will always be more than words. Learning this has been my greatest reward.

This page intentionally left blank

The Guerrilla Sniper Tactics Handbook

Chapter 5

Raids and Ambushes

It is better to be feared then loved, if you cannot be both

Niccolo Machiavelli

Raids and Ambushes

Tactics, Techniques, and Procedures for Successful Operations

On 4 July 1976 one hundred commandos from the Israeli Defense Force conducted a highly successful night hostage rescue at the Entebbe Airport in Uganda. The raid named Operation Entebbe resulted in one hundred and two hostages rescued with only one IDF commando killed, the unit's commander. Israeli transport planes carried the commandos over 2,500 miles from Israel to Uganda for the raid. The operation, which took a week of planning, lasted 90 minutes. At the completion of the raid all the hijackers plus forty-five Ugandan soldiers were dead. In addition to the hostage rescue the IDF commandos destroyed thirty Soviet MiG-17s and MiG-21s belonging to the Ugandan air force.

Many special operations missions fall into the category of either being a raid or an ambush. The primary difference between a raid and an ambush is that in a raid you don't plan to hold the terrain, you just want to cause confusion, capture somebody/destroy something, and then get out, where an ambush is a surprise attack from a concealed position against a moving or temporarily halted target.

The Israeli hostage rescue is a perfect example of a well planned and well executed raid. While both raids and ambushes require deliberate planning and preparation to be successful, a raid is dynamic in nature and the ambush is all about patience.

Every raid and every ambush is unique. Its precise nature is dependent upon the mission, the terrain, the expected enemy force, and the ability of the troops conducting it. However certain characteristics are common to all good raids and ambushes. Both raids and ambushes rely on speed, surprise, and violence of action to be successful. To gain surprise the operation should be conducted at a time and place least expected by the enemy. Darkness, rain, fog, and snow all work to the attacker's advantage. Raids and ambushes conducted in enemy rear areas or from seemingly impassable terrain such as a swamp provide surprise and destroy enemy moral. These "behind the lines" types of attacks can be most deadly because support troops are often not trained in immediate action drills and can be less capable soldiers.

Security is essential to maintaining surprise. Security seals off the objective area and prevents anyone from entering or leaving once the operation starts. They provide the patrol early warning of reinforcements and in the ambush, information as to the size and composition of the enemy entering the ambush site.

The raid or ambush is initiated with the heaviest casualty producing weapon available. Claymore mines are ideal for ambushes while machine guns work well for both raids and ambushes. Both begin with high volumes of accurate deadly fire to achieve fire superiority through surprise and violence of action. Machine guns should be positioned to fire at the maximum amount of the target area and be capable of hitting multiple targets simultaneously (enfilade fire).

In most cases the attack force will assault through the objective, ensuring all occupying enemy are dead, and set up a hasty perimeter on the far side. Specialty teams will then return to the objective to perform their missions. Search teams will then return to the objective to search bodies, vehicles, and buildings. Prisoner teams will secure any live enemy personnel for transport. Demolition team will place and prime charges to destroy anything that cannot be carried by the patrol. Everything should be accomplished in a matter of minutes with many tasks being conducted in unison. Raids and ambushes make a lot of noise and are sure to attract a lot of reinforcements so it is essential to not spend more time on the objective than absolutely necessary.

Once the specialty teams are done, the attack force departs from the objective. Security teams remain in position until all elements of the attack force have left the objective. If available, artillery fire or close air support can be called to fire on the objective to further destroy and hinder pursuit. All elements of the patrol regroup at the objective rally point. Essential information obtained during the operation is disseminated to everyone, this way if one man makes it back to friendly lines the information will be passed on. The patrol then quickly departs the area taking care to conceal their tracks.

The leader of the ambush or raid needs to carefully analyze his Mission, Enemy, Terrain and weather, Troops and support available, Time available, Civil considerations, and Media considerations (METT-TCM) as well as Observation and Fields of Fire, Cover and Concealment, Obstacles (man-made and natural), Key or Decisive Terrain, Avenues of Approach (OCOKA) to determine the best tactics and organization for the patrol. Personnel must be informed as to their duties and rehearsed thoroughly until their actions become instinctive. Control during execution phase is extremely difficult. Troops must be able to perform their duties with a minimum of commands from their leaders. A warning order and detailed operations order are critical for soldiers to understand their role in the mission and the commander's intent.

Ambushes

The primary purpose of an ambush is to kill or capture enemy personnel and his equipment. A secondary purpose is harassment. Frequent ambushes force the enemy to divert men from other missions to protect convoys and troop movements. Ambushing an enemy patrol mean the patrol failed to accomplish whatever mission it was directed to accomplish by their commander. While successful ambushes can greatly degrade a militaries overall mission the secondary affect on individual enemy soldiers is an increase in anxiety degrading their overall moral.

There are three general categories of ambush; Point, Area, and Hasty. A Point ambush is one where forces are deployed to support attack of a single kill zone. Point ambushes often fail to produce heavy casualties especially against guerrillas operating in jungles or other restricted terrain because the enemy will attempt to immediately break contact and escape. An Area ambush is one where forces are deployed at multiple related point ambushes. The idea behind the area ambush is to block escape routes with multiple point ambushes. A Hasty ambush is an immediate action drill it is used when a patrol spots an enemy patrol but it itself is not spotted. The patrol quickly occupies a concealed position along the enemies' route and conducts the ambush when the enemy troops are in the most vulnerable position. The hasty ambush can also be used as a defensive tactic. In the event that the patrol is occupying a security halt and an enemy force is detected they would wait and initiate the attack just as the enemy approaches the position prior to being detected.

Linear Ambush

The linear ambush is the simplest of all the ambushes. It is generally deployed along an enemy route of movement such as a road, trail, or stream. The attack force is positioned parallel to the long axis of the kill zone and then subjects the target to heavy flanking fire. The kill zone is limited by the area which the attack force can effectively cover with a heavy volume of highly concentrated fire. The linear ambush is appropriate in close terrain which restricts the enemy maneuver and in open terrain where one flank is restricted by natural obstacles or can be restricted by mines, demolitions, or mantraps. Obstacles can be placed between the attack force and kill zone to protect against a counter ambush assault. An advantage of the linear ambush is its relative ease in control under all visibility conditions.

L shaped Ambush

A variation of the linear ambush is the L shaped ambush. The long side of the arrack force is parallel to the kill zone and delivers flanking fire. The short end of the attack force is at the end of and at right angles to the kill zone and delivers enfilading fire which interlocks with fire from the other leg. This formation is very flexible. It can be established on a straight stretch of road or trail or at a sharp bend. Fire can be shifted to a parallel the long leg of the enemy attempts to assault or escape. In addition the short leg prevents escape in its direction and reinforcements in its direction. The short leg is an ideal location for heavy weapons such as a machine gun allowing them to fire along the long axis of the kill zone. In vehicle ambushes the lead vehicle can be disabled further blocking the movement in and out of the kill zone.

T Shaped Ambush

The T shaped ambush is known as the bloody nose ambush. It can be used to harass a larger force and slow its movement. The attack force is formed across and at right angles to the enemy's route of movement so that it and the target form a T. When the lead elements of the target are engaged they will normally attempt to maneuver right or left to close with the ambush. Mines, mantraps, or other obstacles to the flank of the kill zone permit the attack force to deliver heavy fire and withdraw without becoming decisively engaged.

Baited Trap Ambush

This approach is used when routes of approach for reinforcements are limited and predictable. A central kill zone is established. Point ambushes are established along routes of approach for reinforcements. The target in the central kill zone serves as the "bait" to lure relieving units into the outlying ambush. Outlying ambushers need not be strong enough to destroy their targets they may be harassing ambushers which eat away at the target by successive contacts. This technique can also use fixed installations as the bait. The attack on the installation may be a genuine raid or it may be a ruse to lure the enemy into the ambush.

Raids

One of the most complex operations a patrol can undertake is the raid. Raid missions should be assigned with an overall objective in mind. Raid missions are intended to achieve precise results on specific targets. Preliminary planning for the raid must include gathering all available intelligence. The patrol leader can then organize his patrol to accomplish specific sub tasks.

The security element is responsible for early warning around the perimeter of the objective area. It is divided into security teams, one team for each security position. The support element provides heavy supportive fire on the objective during the assault. As the assault element takes the objective, the support fires lifts and shifts to engage enemy personnel fleeing the attack. The support element contains the crew served weapons and sniper teams that engage the enemy on the objective. The assistant patrol leader is usually located with the support element to facilitate control. The assault element maneuvers upon and closes with the enemy. This element sweeps across the objective and secures the far side. Specialty teams perform their functions and the assault team withdraws. There are too many variables to establish a hard and fast rule concerning time on the objective but generally speaking for a raid, the less time the better.

Raids are extremely difficult and dangerous. The raid requires a precise application of Speed, Surprise, and Violence of Action to be successful. Fire superiority must be immediate and continuous. Once the raid is initiated the enemy must never have a chance to delay the assault team and prevent them from completing their mission. Precise planning, rehearsals, and dynamic execution increase the likelihood of success.

Training Tips for Raids and Ambushes

The only effective way to train for a raid and ambush is to conduct all training in as realistic training environment as possible. Follow the Crawl-Walk-Run principle starting with basic walk through and ending with full blown live fire exercise in real time. If time allows find a training area that closely matches to target area. Early planning should include a well constructed terrain model based on current reconnaissance.

Fire superiority is not necessarily lots of bullets fired. Bullets must hit their targets. Few people can accurately deliver rounds firing full auto at a moving target at extended distance in combat. The emphasis should be on well aimed shots that eliminate threats and not just forcing the threat to cover. Snipers or designated marksman can often be more effective in suppressing enemy than machineguns especially when they position is concealed and their weapons are suppressed.

Security is an essential aspect of any military operation. The importance for plans being kept secret cannot be overstated. With easy access to smart phones, cameras, and social media, it is too easy for the enemy to find out about operations often from our own troops. There have been numerous tactical operations that have been leaked prior to them being conducted some with catastrophic results. Operations can be easily foiled by seemingly harmless civilians who watch our preparations as they go about their business. Make plans in secret, use deception, and use counter-surveillance where applicable.

Raids and Ambush Definitions

Ambush Force - The patrol, squad, platoon, or other element which establishes the ambush.

Attack Force - The fire and maneuver portion of a point ambush. In a patrol the assault and support element are in the attack force.

Assault Element - The assault element is the part of the patrol that attacks the enemy. It may be made up of special purpose teams and specific high casualty producing weapons teams.

Enfilade - A formation or position is "in enfilade" if weapons fire can be directed along its longest axis. For instance, a trench is enfiladed if the opponent can fire down the entire length of the trench hitting multiple positions. A column of marching troops is enfiladed if fired on from the front or rear such that the projectiles travel the length of the column.

Defilade - A unit or position is "in defilade" if it uses natural or artificial obstacles to shield or conceal. Defilade is also used to refer to a position on the reverse slope of a hill or within a depression in level or rolling terrain. Defiladed positions on hilltops are advantageous because dead space cannot be engaged with direct fire.

Deliberate Action - Deliberate action operations are planned operations that are rehearsed and executed when the team has the highest likelihood of success.

Deliberate Ambush - An Ambush planned as a specific action against a specific target. Because of the time allowed for planning METT-TCM and OAKOC should be used. Detailed information about the route of movement and time that enemy will arrive and depart the area are necessary for planning the ambush.

Far Ambush - An ambush where the attack force is located beyond reasonable assaulting distance from the kill zone. This distance is beyond hand grenade or handgun range. For the sake of the guerrilla sniper this distance should be beyond the effective range of assault rifles.

Hasty Ambush - This ambush is a target of opportunity, often the actions of a search and attack patrol. Used when detailed information is not available. The patrol establishes an ambush in a likely location for enemy movement and ambushes the first suitable target to appear.

Harassing Ambush - An ambush in which the attack is by fire only. The attack force does not close with and finish the enemy. This ambush is meant to hurt the moral of the enemy force and force them to deviate from their assigned mission. This type of far ambush is the primary tactic of the guerrilla sniper.

Immediate Action - Is the type of operation where any time taken for preparation, planning or rehearsal means lives lost. An example of an immediate action would be reacting to an ambush or an active gunman. Immediate action battle drills should be understood and practiced so they are reactive response.

Immediate Action Drills - Drills designed to provide swift and positive small unit reaction to enemy contact. These drills are specific to the unit and the tactics, techniques, and procedures should be closely guarded secret.

Kill Zone - The portion of the ambush site where fires are concentrated to isolate, trap, and destroy the target.

Near Ambush - An ambush where the attack force is located within reasonable assaulting distance from the kill zone (50 meters or less).

Security Force - The early warning and or the security portion of the ambush. Closes off ends of the ambush and prevents escape from the kill zone. Prevents surprise reinforcements by enemy forces.

Rally Point - Is a place where the patrol can assemble and reorganize. Must be free of enemy, provide cover/concealment, and be defensible for short periods of time. The rally point should also be easily recognizable by all patrol members

Objective Rally Point - The rally point most near the objective. It is used to make final preparations, conduct leader reconnaissance, finalize camouflage, and as an assembly/reorganization area immediately after accomplishing the mission.

This page intentionally left blank

Chapter 6

Sniper Tactics and Observation Techniques

There is no avoiding war; it can only be postponed to the advantage of others.

Niccola Machiavelli

Sniper Tactics and Observation Techniques

You can spend all day at the range mastering marksmanship but if you don't learn tactics and learn to think strategically then that skill will have limited use. Being a warrior means training for war and being a sniper means training to hunt and shoot people. Learning to think with strategy takes practice like any other skill. It will likely take decades to understand and a lifetime to master. Study the information in this chapter and use it to see the world through the eyes of a sniper.

Speed

The more factors there are to consider, the more difficult it is to analyze them quickly. Knowing what to focus on and what can be ignored is crucial. Speed comes from the ability to do this. Remove everything you don't need. What is left is fast and efficient.

The O-O-D-A Loop

Colonel John Boyd, U.S. Air Force (Retired) 1927-1997, conceived a four-step system to guide the prosecution of military operations to swift, ultimate victory. Boyd called this system the O-O-D-A loop. "O-O-D-A" is an acronym that stands for observe, orient, decide, and act. These are sequential activities that guide snipers to effective decisions. The act portion creates a new round of observations, followed by a second cycle of orientation, decision, and action. Boyd suggested that individuals or groups that could cycle through these four steps faster than their adversaries had a tactical advantage

Observe

Observation, the first step in the O-O-D-A loop, is a search for information such as the baseline. The information that should be sought is the tactical situation. Only slightly less urgent is what Boyd called "outside information." This could include the environment; the behavior and tendencies of the enemy; the physical, mental, and moral situation, etc

It must be emphasized that this is not a passive step. It requires an active effort to seek out all the available information by whatever means possible.

What you're looking for is data that doesn't fit with your baseline. It is these <u>differences</u> that offer the potential for learning something that your enemies don't know, thereby creating a tactical advantage that you can exploit. Something as simple as a winter coat being worn on a hot day that can give us clues to an attack that is about to happen.

Orient

Orient is the decision maker in the O-O-D-A loop. Our orientation to the world shapes the decisions we make, the actions we take, and what we choose to observe. Orientation is formed from many factors, including cultural traditions, previous experiences and new information based on what's going on right now. These are then combined into a new, updated baseline. To the extent the sniper is able to develop a more accurate picture than his or her opponent, the quality of his decisions and effectiveness of actions improve, sometimes dramatically. Orientation drives everything else. The faster we can orient ourselves, the better and more effective observations, decisions, and actions will be.

Decide

The decide step is conscious choice of predetermined list of battle plans. Understanding the threat and choosing between pre determined plans is critical because we don't want to make complicated plans while in combat. Having pre determined battle plans is a desirable situation, because it speeds the cycle time of the O-O-D-A loop. Battle plans should be conceived when we are calm and take into consideration the law and the morality of our actions. Our battle plans should counter our enemies the most likely and most deadly courses of action. Have a plan A and a plan B.

Act

Action is the whole reason for going through the O-O-D-A steps in the first place. This is why we train for scenarios and develop battle plans. This is the part where we put the battle plan into action. It is crucial to keep in mind that the very action we take will influence the environment in which we act. The environment will change. This changes our orientation, or baseline, to some degree. The quicker we realize that this change is developing, the sooner we can adjust our orientation to more closely estimate the new baseline and act again.

Observation

Snipers must establish and maintain the initiative on enemy forces. The initiative is achieved and maintained though surprise and by staying undetected. This is accomplished by being properly trained, proper use of equipment, understanding the nature of your enemy, and actively seeking them. The sniper must keep the enemy reacting to them so they do not have the ability to organize a counter attack.

Developing observation skills enables the sniper to attain and maintain relevant situational awareness in order to locate and engage enemy targets. Anything or anyone that you observe in your immediate vicinity that is unusual, out of place, or out of context, should be viewed as potentially dangerous, until you have had a chance to assess it. It is a threat until it is proven otherwise.

Establishing a Baseline

A baseline is the reference point against which other things can be evaluated. Cultures, neighborhoods, environments, and individuals all have baselines. To be useful, a baseline has to have everything in its natural or normally occurring state. Everything has a baseline. A baseline is established with the first look. As you observe an area / person / location more, you will continue to refine and improve your baseline. Look for disturbances to the baseline and identify anything that is different, abnormal, peculiar or not easily classified. Establish a basis for comparison. A baseline is established over time through repetitious levels of observation to establish a routine of human nature, environmental patterns, and animal behaviors. Establishing a baseline and assessing the threat is often an educated guess. You may not always be right, but you are not always wrong either.

Cultural Baselines

Cultural baselines will be developed at a national, regional, and local level. Every culture has baseline, a neighborhood has baseline, and an environment has a baseline. Sounds, odors, colors, and textures all have baselines. Monitor the baseline closely and look for items that stand out or are not normal when compared to this baseline. Specifically look for:

- What is there that shouldn't be there?
- What is not "there" that should be?

The national baseline is derived from knowledge of religious holidays, secular holidays, normal workweek, weekends, political, and historical events.

- Holidays where shops and schools will be closed
- National Elections

Regional baselines are built upon national baselines with added regional emphasis on religious holidays, secular holidays, customs, and sectarian observances

- Geographical relevance (southern marshes vs. western desert)

- Societal norms (clothing fashions, hygiene, men and women's place in society)

Regional wealth and resources affect local baselines. Local baselines are often driven by community events. Religious practices and business customs will make establishing easier because they usually follow a set schedule. Schools, weather, agricultural resources and methods, all influence development of the local baseline.

- Business practices
- School hours
- Wildlife
- Material wealth
- Architecture and villages
- Tribal customs (style of governance, familial relations, etc.)
- Environmental impacts (heat, cold, rain, day activities, night activities, etc.)
- Availability of infrastructure (roads, electricity, sewage, etc.)

By understanding the national, regional, and local baselines the sniper can develop their understanding of the norms and react accordingly to deviations within the baseline.

Snipers attempt to blend into the local baseline in order to prevent detection. Deviations from the baseline could be an indicator that something is wrong. Shops closing early, the lack of children playing, lack of police, the number of people attending religious services, and bizarre animal behaviors are great examples in the change of the baseline. If a sniper is not familiar with the locals and the environment then these example changes would go unnoticed.

Observe actions of the local populace. Most communities are tight knit through relatives and a social network. They usually know that a preplanned attack will occur. If you arrive and the locals scatter, some offensive action by the enemy will probably occur. This observation can be used with the local police or army. If they are not at their usual posts or patrols, this is a key indicator that enemy action is likely. This higher level of enemy activity requires a heightened situational awareness by the sniper. They must scan all areas in their assigned sector, as urban terrain presents an environment that provides many additional locations for a sniper to hide.

Elements of Visual Perception

Eyesight is the primary means by which to gather, organize and interpret information. There are elements of visual perception that allow us to detect target indicators when looking for targets, threats and disturbances to a baseline.

Movement

Movement is a large factor because the human eye is strongly attracted to any movement during both day and night. A movement will attract your attention so that you can carefully study the area to detect a potential threat. The peripheral vision is more tuned to movement so not looking directly at something sometimes make movement easier to detect.

- Primary movement is movement of the actual "target".
- Secondary movement is from the target indicator.

Color

This is the result of differing qualities of the light reflected or emitted by an object. Much of this depends on the quality of the existing light. Objects in conditions of reduced visibility often appear in shades of gray.

Shape

This is something that is distinguished from its surroundings by its outline and contour. When lines and edges come together an outline is created. We perceive the outline as a shape. This is the key factor in its recognition.

- Unless broken up by camouflage, a familiar shape such as a man, vehicle, or weapon can be rapidly seen, even at a great distance.

Line, Outline and Edge

All objects, especially those that are man-made, have a line or edge to them.

- This line and edge often leads to an outline of an object (straight lines, sharp angles, smooth curves, etc.).

- The untrained individual may see a line or edge, but the trained individual will be able to see the outline.

Contrast

Contrast is the difference between entities or objects being compared.

- Look for a contrast that does not match the current environment.
- Consider background and foreground.

Texture

Texture is the distinctive physical composition or structure of something, especially with respect to the size, shape, and arrangements of its parts, appearance and feel of a surface.

- The texture that you will notice will not resemble the environment (and background).
- Consider texture such as dead vegetation, new paint, or improved construction of walls.

Light – Reflecting, Sunlight and Shadows

Flat surfaces normally reflect light and rough surfaces normally absorb light. Light also impacts colors and the value of colors.

- At times a shadow shows up better than the object itself, especially from a high vantage point. When scanning an area, pay particular attention to shadows.
- Not many people pay attention to their own shadow. They may be utilizing cover and concealment well, but are completely exposed by their shadow.

Positive Space

Positive space is space that is taken up by solid objects such as buildings, trees, signs, and vehicles. Typically, you cannot shoot or see through positive space. The human eye will naturally move from positive space to positive space as the eye is attracted to this. For example, in tree lines, your eyes are attracted to trunks and prominent branches.

Negative Space

This is space between positive spaces. This is the "nothing" that the human eye subconsciously does not recognize or consider. A good sniper will try to operate in the negative spaces when feasible. Good camouflage resembles negative space.

Remember: Any technique you use to locate and expose a sniper can be used in reverse to find you.

Observation Techniques

Scan Patterns

Scanning techniques are the same for both naked eye and aided vision (optics). It is important to scan the entire scene with the naked eye before using your optics. Using just your eyes, scan an area fast - look for movement, shine, shadows. Always scan right to left. In our culture, our brains are conditioned to read left-to-right. When you force your brain to scan in the opposite direction, you are more apt to focus in on things that stand out from the expected baseline.

Do not focus on one particular place. Your peripheral vision is diminished by concentrating on a particular spot or range as you scan. When you scan with optics try to hover slightly over areas where the enemy is likely to be.

Do a very slow and detailed scan. Do not spend more than a few minutes with optics to your eyes. "Relax" your eyes by lowering your optics and focusing on a distant then a close point a few times. Look at shadows. A person standing behind a building, tree or rock may be completely out of sight but may have a clear shadow that gives him away.

Obstacle "Burn Through"

Learn how to "burn through" bushes and other obstacles by looking beyond the obstacle, or through it if possible. Adjust your focus to a point beyond the bushes, woods, etc. Adjust focus until you can see clearly through the obstacle. Give yourself the opportunity to see if there is something within or behind the obstacle.

Shadows

Look deep into shadows with optics. If looking into a dark space, such as a room (door or window), don't focus just on the entrance of the room. Change your focus to look into or through the whole room to the back.

- Snipers can and often do hide in the back of a shadowed area.
- When focusing on the shadowed area, look for the slightest movement or glimpse of a light or reflection.

Combat Profiling

Combat Profiling is the technique of observing an environment for context and relevance. It forms the basis for making determinations on the current situation (either good or bad) by disturbances / anomalies to the baseline. Combat profiling is a learned technique that can be used to detect criminals, insurgents, and terrorists that are hiding within a civilian population. It utilizes habits, routines, demographics, and body language to conduct assessments and make comparisons to the base line to answer the question of <u>why</u> something is out of the ordinary.

Habits and Routines

Humans are habitual; i.e., behavior patterns can be measured, and observed. The enemy will unconsciously follow repeatable, predictable human behavior patterns that can be studied.

Demographics

People familiar with an area act, walk, and drive differently than those who are unfamiliar. People tend to commit crimes and acts of terrorism within an area they are most knowledgeable and comfortable.

Body Language

Body language is the non-verbal movements we make as a part of how we communicate, from waving hands to involuntary twitching of facial muscles. Watch people and learn to read their body language, be aware of falling into the trap of reading stand-alone individual gestures. Most people can tell when a person on a cellular telephone call is in a casual conversation versus an argumentative conversation. However, certain cultures are more animated than others. That conversation could simply be the normal pattern for that person. This could be a stand-alone gesture. Seek context. The same basic principle works for a threat.

If driving past a bus stop, most people will look at military personnel, whether with hate, admiration, or wonder; you need to focus on the person <u>not</u> looking. Look for the people who are trying hard to blend in Professional bad guys hide in plain sight, in order to blend with regular people. However, the regular people will act differently toward a stranger. Look for the body language of each person approaching a vehicle checkpoint (VCP), entry checkpoint (ECP) or your patrol.

Anyone who exhibits characteristics that fall well <u>above</u> or <u>below</u> your baseline needs to be immediately segregated. You may discover that he is just an emotionally disturbed person or you may have stopped a suicide bomber. The key is using observation skills to increase situational awareness through the use of context and relevance as it relates to a specific area of operation. Combat profiling depends on individual behavior that is outside of the norm for an area.

The benefits of combat profiling include:

- Increased observation skills
- Increased situational awareness
- Enhanced ability for mission accomplishment
- Increased ability to determine friend from the enemy
- Increased lethality

Combat profiling works on people, vehicles, and events. It will work in any culture.

Employment of Combat Profiling

The first step of combat profiling is establishing a baseline for your AO so you can look for indicators based on known or predicted enemy methods of operation. Deviations are anomalies that stand out from your baseline of behavior and conduct, and can be identified. If you can identify a method of operation (MO), you can identify a threat. Identification can lead to interruption. If the enemy has his plan interrupted, he may not execute it. Combat profiling is *always* proactive. Here are examples of enemy activities; awareness of these can enable us to recognize a threat and to act:

- Tracking movements of important leadership and potential key local targets.
- Gathering intelligence and surveying their target areas; examples are ECPs, FOBs, and VCPs.

In a large percent of recently studied terrorist incidents, there were observable preparatory acts prior to the incident. Combat profiling could have identified these pre-incident behaviors.

- Rehearsing enemy operations. This is observable. Watch for trends from repeated actions.
- New sneakers on a suspected enemy can be an observable characteristic above the baseline.
- Gathering the necessary tools such as mobile phone bases / batteries / fuel / IED material.
- Training and rehearsals may include suspicious drive-bys / suspicious people attempting to gain entrance to VCP / ECPs.
- Building a plan that allows them to execute and then flee. Potential entrances and escape routes reconnoitered for future enemy operations.

Human Behavior

These are the emotional and physical states that develop the mood of the environment. Surveying the area, reading human disposition, noticing routine and nature give you foresight to enemy activity. Sometimes a change in the baseline is not obvious. An individual is on a cell phone in the shadows next to the shop on the corner. You notice him and pick up your optics to get a better look. This individual is nervous looking, by himself, wearing running shoes (everyone else is wearing sandals), constantly looking at the police station, and looks away when he notices you observing him with optics.

Animal Behavior

Wild animals have a tendency toward the "fight or flight" instinct when threatened. A wild animal will normally leave the area unless it feels trapped or directly threatened. Domesticated animals have a tendency to migrate toward human interaction and are naturally curious of things out of the ordinary. Observe the activities of local wildlife. Any birds or animals may be good indicators. Domesticated animals can also be indicators. If a dog walking in the street stops and looks up, this is abnormal behavior for a dog. Try to see what caused him to look up. Likewise, if a group of goats are staring at a rubble pile, people might be behind it.

Environmental Patterns

Remove animal and human factors from the situation and ask:

- What is the natural state of the landscape such as vegetation growth, rock formations?
- What is the weather (wind, rain, temperature, etc.) and what are its effects?

Intelligence Reporting Format

S – Size

A – Activity

L – Location

U – Uniform/Unit

T – Time and Date

E – Equipment

S – Size

What is the size of the unit?

Number of personnel

Number of vehicles (highway, rail, etc.)

A – Activity

What are they doing?

L – Location

Where are they located?

— Grid coordinates

U – Uniform/Unit

What are they wearing?

What unit do they belong to?

T – Time and Date

What time of day/night do you see them?

— Day and time group (DTG)

— Zulu or local

E – Equipment

What type of equipment did you see?

Chapter 7

Understanding Wind and Determining Unknown Ranges

Whosever desired constant success must change his conduct with the times.

Noccolo Machiavelli

Understanding Wind and Determining Unknown Ranges

Compensating for wind is essential for a sniper

One of the elements that affect a sniper more than any other is the wind. It is vital to understanding the effect the wind has on the bullet during the flight so you can make the proper adjustment to your weapon to successfully hit your target.

Determining wind direction is the first step towards making the correct calculation. These are called wind values. There are three basic wind values:

1. **Zero value wind-** is wind that is blowing directly towards or away from the shooter so the path of the bullet is parallel to the path of the wind.
2. **Half value wind-** is wind that is blowing at a 45 degree angle right to left or left to right of the target.
3. **Full value wind-** is wind that is blowing straight across or at a 90 degree angle horizontally left to right or right to left.

The next step is to determine the speed of the wind. This can be done in many ways. Small wind gauges are available and they do an excellent job. Traditional or low tech ways are to look at the effect the wind has on tree, grasses, bushes, mirage, and range flags.

Example:

1-3 MPH wind can barely be felt on your face

3-5 MPH wind is felt lightly on your face

5-8 MPH wind will cause leaves to stay in constant motion

8-12 MPH wind will cause dust and paper to rise

12-15 MPH wind will cause small trees to sway

15-20 MPH wind will cause small trees to bend

20-25 MPH wind will cause tall grasses to lie down and large trees to sway

The key to reading the wind is to practice every chance you get. A couple of hints most people tend to overestimate wind speed, be conservative. When shooting at longer ranges beyond 200 yards check wind direction and speed of objects ¾ of the way to the target and use the mirage as an indicator of the wind speed and direction.

Once you have determined the wind speed and direction you are ready to make your calculation. The formula for determine how much wind adjustment to put on your scope is:

Wind Velocity X Distance divided by the factor for your particular bullet.

308 Caliber 168 grain bullets

$$\underline{V\ 15\ X\ D\ 2\ (200) = 30}$$

$$15 = 2\ MOA$$

5.56 55 grain bullet

$$\underline{V15\ X\ D2\ (200) = 30}$$

$$10 = 3\ MOA$$

Ranging; the Strategy for Success

For a sniper to ever be successful regardless of how good of a shot he is accurately estimating the range between the shooter and the target and making the correct adjustment is essential. The sniper can accurately estimate the wind and be a master of the fundamentals of marksmanship but an inaccurate range adjustment will likely cause him to miss the target. The Sniper needs to use all the tools at his disposal to quickly and accurately estimate unknown distances.

With the advent of **Laser Range Finders** (LRFs) determining unknown distances has never been easier or more accurate. Prior to any range session or mission the LRF should be inspected and the batteries replaced. Spare batteries should also be included in the mission required equipment list. Not all LRFs use batteries the same so the number of spare batteries carried should be based on experience with the equipment. When using the LRF to determine the range to a target, its best to verify that there is nothing obstructing the view of the target like branches, windows, or fences because they will give an inaccurate reading. It's also best to take multiple readings of the same target to verify the accuracy of the first reading. While having a LRF is essential equipment for the sniper also knowing how to determine range by other means is critical in the event the LRF becomes inoperable or the target is otherwise obscured.

One simple method for determining an unknown range is **Partner Averaging**. The partner averaging method is when the sniper and spotter both looking at the same target each make their best guess at the distance and taking an average of the two. If a sniper thought a target was 200 but his spotter thought it was 150 then they would agree on 175 and likely a hit would most likely result. The partner averaging method requires practice and works best at ranges closer than 400 but is very quick and surprisingly accurate. When a sniper is deployed to a new area of operation he must determine the size and shapes of common objects. Doors, windows, street signs, height of curbs, average height of the enemy, and common sizes of military equipment will allow him to use those known sizes to determine unknown distances. By simply knowing the size of a window the sniper can use the **mil relation formula** to determine the distance to the window before a target presents itself greatly reducing the time to make calculations and adjustments prior to firing at the target.

Mil relation formula

$$\frac{\text{Target size (inches)} \times 27.77}{\text{Mil Reading of Target}} = \text{Distance to the target in yards}$$

$$\frac{\text{Target size (inches)} \times 25.4}{\text{Mil Reading of Target}} = \text{Distance to the target in meters}$$

Remember: An effective sniper will use every available tool to determine unknown ranges likely using multiple techniques on a single mission.

This page is intentionally left blank

The Guerrilla Sniper Tactics Handbook

Chapter 8

Sniper/ Counter Sniper Tactics Techniques Procedures

The fist method of estimating the intelligence of a ruler is to look at the men around him.

Niccolo Machiavelli

Sniper/ Counter Sniper Tactics Techniques and Procedures

It's been said that it takes a sniper to kill a sniper. The reason a sniper is so hard to kill is because a true sniper is a highly trained professional that stacks the deck in his favor making killing him difficult. History has shown that a single well trained rifleman can change history and well trained sniper can bring an army to a halt. To defeat your enemy you have to understand him. Mess that up and your replacement will have to deal with it. Study the enemy sniper and try to see what he sees, try to think like he thinks, and try to move like he moves.

Enemy Sniper definition and capability assessment

Specially Trained Sniper

The most dangerous sniper is one who has been specially selected, trained, and equipped with an accurate sniper rifle outfitted with modern scopes, night vision, and even thermal imagers. He is an expert trained to select key individuals as his targets. He can hit at great ranges (sometimes out to 1,000 meters) and is skilled in avoiding detection. This sniper is the most difficult to counter effectively.

Trained Marksman

A trained marksman is a common sniper often found in urban combat. He is a skilled soldier, equipped with a standard-issue weapon, who is an above-average shot. He normally has fair-to-good field craft skills and is difficult to detect in the urban environment. He might be employed independently or in a team to create confusion among friendly forces, cause casualties, or harass and disrupt the tempo of operations. He can be found in fairly large numbers in the armies of many potential adversaries.

Armed Irregulars

This sniper might have little or no formal military training but might have experience in urban combat. He might wear a distinguishing uniform and might even appear to be merely another of the thousands of noncombatants found in a large urban area. He might carry his weapon openly and might go to great lengths to avoid identification as a sniper. His strengths are his knowledge of the local terrain and his ability to melt into the local populace.

Sniper Counter Sniper Tactics, Techniques, and Procedures

Proactive Tips

- Maintain 360° security.
- DON'T SET PATTERNS.
- Deny enemy use of over watching terrain.
- Remove rank insignia and do not salute in the field in accordance with area of operation (AO) guidance/local policy.
- Don't stand out; everyone should look the same.
- Use observation posts (OPs) and ground and aerial sensor platforms.
- Use magnified optics to scan for snipers.
- Use small recon and security patrols. Limit exposure; move quickly and use cover and concealment.
- "Slice the Pie, Reduce Exposure"
- Wear protective armor.
- Use armored vehicles.
- Erect shields/screens for cover/concealment.
- Use smoke hazes or smoke screens to obscure the sniper's field of view and limit the effectiveness of his fire.

- Stick to the shadows; use cover and concealment
- Increase/change your security posture after 20 minutes in one location and continue to change/upgrade.
- Use interpreters with radio on scan to pick up enemy communications.
- Use cover and concealment whenever possible,
- Stop and search suspicious vehicles seen driving by more than once.
- Plan to use roving vehicles that can flex to investigate suspicious vehicles.
- Keep personnel in CONSTANT motion, walking in "W" and "S" patterns.
- Use intelligence, surveillance, and reconnaissance assets.
- Keep vehicles available for searches.

The best place to start looking for an enemy sniper

Focus searches around 25–200 meters first. It is possible for "specially trained snipers" to engage at farther ranges but less likely that they will be successful at farther ranges. In rural areas search distances are often farther.

Reaction to a sniper Attack

- Take up covered/concealed positions (also conceal with SMOKE).
- Any wounded soldier applies "self aid."
- Identify sniper location and return fire.
- Find the sniper by his mistakes: reflections, dust clouds, muzzle flashes, etc.
- Insert a cleaning rod in a bullet hole to indicate the bullet's path and possible point of origin.
- Cordon most likely area (25- to 200- meter radius from your position).
- Hunt down and KILL the enemy sniper.

Enemy Tactics Techniques and Procedures

- Deliberate: well planned, resourced Hasty: targets of opportunity
- Urban attacks are usually 25–200 meters from street or elevated positions
- Rural attacks are usually from longer ranges
- The enemy sniper will wait to take follow-on shots on medics or rescuers
- Enemy attacks are videotaped for propaganda/ training/after action reviews
- Might operate as part of a team using multiple shooting positions

- Might use prepared vehicle shooting platform like the "D.C. Sniper"
- Vehicles might be marked in a way that allows passage through co-opted checkpoints
- Might attempt to assess success by driving or walking by the target after the shot
- Might use "bait" (i.e., a dead body or IED) to draw friendly forces into his "kill zone"
- Will engage the easiest target, such as a top gunner or stationary guard— KEEP MOVING!
- Will aim for vulnerable areas or aim to miss body armor
- Will attack mostly during daylight hours
- Enemy TTPs can and will change.

Tactics for Defense against Enemy Snipers

Pre Patrol

- Conduct pre-patrol brief using the
- 5-paragraph operations order format.
- Highlight current Intel and enemy tactics, techniques, and procedures (TTPs).

- Rehearse battle drills.

On Patrol

- Maintain 360° security.
- Limit stationary time.
- Limit exposure.
- Respond quickly and aggressively.
- Find, fix, and finish.
- Everyone is a counter-sniper.
- Use optics to "out-look" the enemy.
- Use improvised or field-expedient technology (e.g., nets, screens, etc.) Immediately.

Post-patrol

- Conduct detailed patrol debriefing.
- Follow through (you did find, fix, and finish; now exploit and analyze)

Use of Mannequins

Mannequins have been used in war since ancient times. As far back as the Chinese dynasties, whole divisions of mannequins and campfires were used to deceive opponents' spies. In the current conflict, the use of mannequins is again becoming commonplace. Mannequins are being fielded in greater numbers. The enemy OODA loop can be hampered by the use of mannequins in guard towers and vehicles. Placing mannequins in areas where snipers are likely to shoot can expose snipers and make them unsure.

Correct use of mannequins is not only to dress them properly for the mission, but to have natural body movement as well. A rotation plan of mannequins and personnel needs to be developed so observers will not become used to stationary mannequins and disregard it. Much like other decoys, in order to draw out snipers, the mannequin must be as real as possible. The Soldier emplacing the mannequin must have a covering/observation plan. Once this happens, battle drills will need to be executed to kill or detain the enemy snipers.

This page intentionally left blank

Chapter 9

Survival, Evasion, and Recovery

Even the side of the mountain there is a road.

Afghan Proverb

Survival, Evasion, and Recovery

Survival skills are critical to the Sniper because snipers often work behind enemy lines in small groups without additional support. The snipers ability to stay hidden can mean the difference between mission success and failure and whether the sniper can return to friendly lines unharmed. Elements of Survival, Evasion, and Recovery should be implemented into every sniper mission.

Evasion Tactics Techniques and Procedures

Immediate Action- Think before you act
- Assess the immediate situation.
- Assess medical condition; treat as necessary.
- Take action to protect from chemical, biologic, radiological, and nuclear hazards.
- Gather equipment, move to initial hole-up/hide site.

- Make initial radio contact in accordance with (IAW) combat search and rescue/special instructions (CSAR/SPINS).
- Sanitize uniform of compromising information.
- Apply initial personal camouflage.

Initial Movement

- Move in the direction of your evasion plan of action (EPA), if possible.
- Attempt to break line of sight from your initial isolating area and move uphill if possible.
- Move out of area, zigzag pattern recommended.
- Use terrain and concealment to your advantage.
- Move to hole up/hide site.

Hole-up/hide site

Select hole up-site/hide site that provides:

- Concealment from ground and air searches
- Safe distance from enemy positions and lines of communications (LOCs)
- Listening and observing points.
- Multiple avenues of escape.

- Protection from the environment.
- Communication/signaling.

Things to do in the hide

- Drink water, treat injuries for long term.
- Evaluate combat needs.
- Inventory equipment.
- Review and execute your escape plan
- Clean and maintain weapons/ equipment.
- Determine specific location.
- Improve camouflage.
- Stay alert, maintain security, and be flexible.

Evasion movement

- Travel slowly and deliberately (you are more at risk during movement)
- Do not leave evidence of travel.
- Use noise and light discipline.
- Stay away from roads and people
- Stop, look, smell, and listen.

- Move from one point of concealment to another point of concealment
- Use evasion movement techniques

Recovery

- Prepare for conventional or unconventional recovery.
- Select best area and prepare for use of communication and signaling device.
- Prepare to transmit position (range and bearing).
- Select site(s) IAW criteria in theater recovery plans.
- Observe/report enemy activity and hazards.
- Secure equipment.
- Stay concealed until recovery is imminent.
- During recovery
- Follow recovery force instructions
    1. Secure weapon
    2. Assume non-threatening posture
    3. Beware of rotors/propellers

Tips for Successful Evasion

Follow these guidelines for successful evasion.

- Keep the positive attitude.
- Use established procedures.
- Follow your plan.
- Maintain radio discipline.
- Be patient.
- Drink water (do not eat food without water).
- Conserve strength.
- Rest and sleep as much as possible.
- Stay out of sight.
- Avoid food, perfumes, or any other odors that may stand out and give you way away.
- Mask scent using natural materials such as dirt or vegetation.

Camouflage

Camouflage patterns should match environment.

- Face- use dark colors on high spots and light colors on any remaining exposed areas. Use a hat, netting, or mask if available.
- Ears- The inside and the backs should have two colors to break up outlines if not covered.
- Head, neck, hands, and under chin. Use a scarf, collar, vegetation, netting, or coloration methods. Try to disguise the shape of the head.
- Light colored hair/ no hair. Give special attention to conceal with scarf or mosquito net.

Position and movement camouflage
- Avoid unnecessary movement
- Take advantage of natural concealment
- Do not over camouflage
- Remember when using shadows, they shift with the sun.
- Never expose shiny objects (watches, pens, glasses)
- Ensure watch alarms and hourly chimes are turned off
- Remove unit patches, name tags, rank insignia, and so forth.

- Break up the outline of the body "V" of the crotch/armpits, head/shoulders.
- Observe from a prone and concealed position.

Shelters

Tips for constructing shelters

- Use camouflage and concealment
- Choose an area with observable approach and escape
- Locate carefully- remember the acronym: BLISS

B - Blend (blend with environment)

L - Low silhouette (smaller than surroundings)

I - Irregular shape (natural looking)

S - Small (enough for you and your gear)

S- Secluded location (least likely to be searched)

Use brush, ridges, ditches, and rocks to keep from forming paths to hole-up/hide site.

- Be wary of natural hazards such as flash floods in ravines and canyons.
- Conceal with minimal to no preparation

- Ensure overhead concealment.
- Attempt to return the area to its original state before you start your movement.

Survival and Evasion movement

Movement tactics and tips

- A moving object is easy to spot. If travel is necessary go slow.
- Try to only move during low light, bad weather, wind, or reduced activity.
- Stay off the ridgelines; use the military crest (2/3 of the way up the hill) to a avoid silhouetting.
- At irregular intervals <u>stop</u> at a point of concealment then: <u>Look</u>, <u>listen</u>, and <u>smell</u>.
- Mask with natural cover
- Camouflage evidence of travel. Route selection requires detailed planning and special techniques (irregular route/zigzag pattern).

Movement techniques

- Do not break braches, leaves, or grass. Use a walking stick to part vegetation and push it back into its original position.
- Do not grab small trees or brush. (This may scuff the bark or create movement that is easily spotted. In the snow country, this creates a path of snowless vegetation.

- Pick firm footing Try Not To:
    1. Overturn ground cover, rocks, and sticks.
    2. Scuff bark on logs and sticks
    3. Make noise by breaking sticks (cloth wrapped around feet helps muffle noise)
    4. Mangle grass and bushes that normally spring back.

- Mask unavoidable tracks in soft footing
    1. Place tracks in the shadows of vegetation, downed logs, and snowdrifts
    2. Move before and during precipitation: allow tracks to fill in.
    3. Travel during windy periods

4. Take advantage of solid surfaces leaving less evidence of travel
- Secure trash and loose equipment: hide or bury discarded items.
- If pursued by dogs concentrate on defeating the handler.
    1. Travel downwind of the dog/handler if possible
    2. Travel over rough terrain and/or through dense vegetation to slow the handler.
    3. Travel downstream through fast moving water.

Obstacles

Penetrate obstacles as follows:

- Enter ditches feet fist to avoid injury.
- Go around chain link and wire fences. Go under fence if avoidable, crossing at damaged areas. Do Not touch fence: look for electrical insulators or security devices.
- Penetrate rail fences, passing under or between lower rails. If this is impractical, go over the top, presenting as low a silhouette as possible.
- Cross roads after observation from concealment to determine enemy activity. Cross at points offering concealment such as bushes, shadows,

or bend in road. Cross in a manner leaving footprints parallel to the road (do this by stepping sideways).

- Use same method of observation for railroad tracks as used for roads. Then, lower your body to the ground aligning parallel to the tracks with face down. Cross the tracks using a semi-pushup motion sideways. WARNING be aware that three rails one may be electrified.

Urban considerations:

- Look for and move to Friendly controlled and location stronghold point.
- Avoid movement into market type and areas and crowds.
- Avoid high rise buildings.
- Head to concealment to break visual contact.
- If seen change direction radically.
- Use caution when passing windows and doors, try to avoid.
- Use cloth, rags, clothing, and other man made material to blend in,
- Conceal movement utilizing buildings, rubble, and other structures.
- Observe structures for movement or life threatening obstacles.

Chapter 10

Handgun Selection for the Sniper

If an injury needs to be done to a man it should be so severe that his vengeance need not be feared.

Niccolo Machiavelli

Handgun Selection for the Sniper

A handgun to a sniper is the last line of defense capable of keeping the enemy beyond arms reach. Things would have gone terribly wrong for a sniper armed only with a pistol to be engaged in a running gunfight with multiple enemy soldiers. Add in the additional stress of magazine changes, retrieving those magazines from unfamiliar places, and the situation would likely end in capture, torture, and death for the sniper. Now a sniper knows that proper field craft and tactics will prevent his handgun from being used to save his life but that same sniper also knows Mr. Murphy's number one law "what can go wrong will go wrong". So a sniper must choose his equipment wisely and then train as he plans to fight with that equipment.

Many factors should go into choosing a proper defensive handgun with caliber being the first. The industry standard for a defensive caliber choice is 9mm, 40 S+W, or 45 ACP. It's my recommendation that at least one of these three calibers should be used. Any variation from the above could make obtaining large quantities of training ammunition difficult for the sniper.

The next consideration should be magazine capacity. I have always been a fan of the 1911 but I do see the advantage of higher capacity magazines in that a larger amount of ammunition can be carried in fewer magazines (15 round magazines as opposed to 8 round magazines). Higher magazine capacity translates to fewer manipulations (magazine changes) while engaging multiple targets. Fewer manipulations in combat are a good thing when your heart rate nears 200 beats per minute and the fine motor capability of the fingers and hands get diminished. Any pistol used for defense should be 100% reliable with hollow point ammunition. Most modern handguns have achieved this type of reliability but do require a break in period of about 500 rounds.

Maintenance and repairs are important considerations because parts do wear out and guns do break. Spare parts should be kept on hand either with the end user or with an armorer if that support is available. Preventative maintenance of a defensive handgun can't be overstated. Guns should be cleaned, inspected, and lubricated prior to and after every operation as well as a complete tear down cleaning and inspection by a competent armorer every six months or sooner if the weapon is subjected to harsh environments. Ammunition should also be rotated frequently.

Holsters used by a sniper are different than those used for other operations. The priorities for the sniper are to protect the handgun and not lose it. The holsters that I have found to be a best compromise of speed and security is the drop leg flap holsters made by both Eagle and Blackhawk Industries. They both feature a thumb break and full flap covering all but the base of the magazine. With the addition of a lanyard attached to the butt of the weapon the gun can only be lost due to severe operator error.

Due consideration should be given to magazine carriers as well as the holster. Several holsters allow mounting magazines directly to the holster. While this choice of carrying a spare magazine makes for more difficult magazine changes with the support hand having to reach so far across the body, but it does ensure that at least a few magazines would be available if a majority of the Sniper's gear was abandoned or damaged.

Once the weapon, holster, and magazine carrier are chosen it's time to begin training. It has been said that it takes 1000 repetitions for something to become a reflex. I recommend at least 1000 draw strokes and presentations to begin developing the required "muscle memory" to be able to defend one's life with a handgun. Once the muscle memory has begun to take effect then move onto live fire with emphasis on the fundamentals of marksmanship. Proper sight alignment, sight picture, trigger press, and trigger reset will ensure that every round fired in anger is a hit. It's been said that "you can't miss fast enough to win a gunfight" and a Sniper surely can't afford to miss any of these critical shots. A sniper should give his handgun selection the same consideration as every other piece of equipment and pick his handgun like his life depended on the choice.

This page intentionally left blank

Chapter 11

Guide to Global Positioning Systems

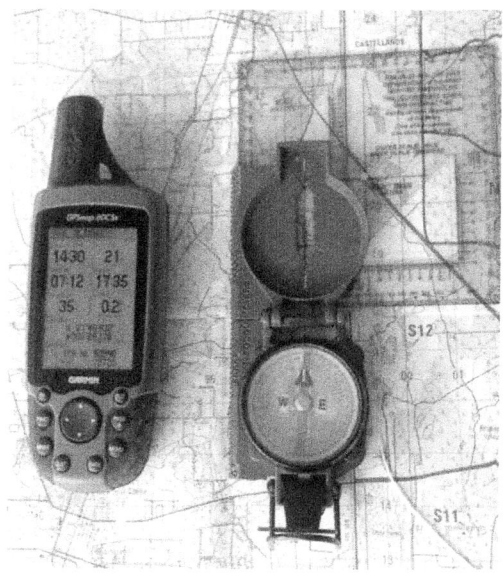

Nearly all men can stand adversity, but if you want to test a man's character give him power.

yep, see what it did to: ~~Abraham Lincoln~~

The Snipers Guide to Global Positioning Systems

Field craft and survival skills are important to the guerrilla sniper conducting operations in hostile terrain. Knowing how to use a map, compass, and terrain association are critical skills for navigation, identifying the guerrilla snipers location, and the target's location. A Global Positioning Systems in the hands of the guerrilla sniper is a force multiplier for situational awareness, intelligence collection, and range estimation. The GPS uses batteries and requires some training but it ranks really high on my list of "really nice to have" equipment therefore it is worthy of being included here.

The GPS receiver is an often misunderstood and underutilized tool for precise navigation. I have seen on several occasions people retrieve a GPS receiver from their backpack, turn in on and wait for it to give them insight on their location only to become frustrated when it does not magically find their way home. I too have been guilty of this kind of thinking because I walked around for many years owning one without a solid grasp on how to use it. It was when I was in Kathmandu 2012 teaching Nepalese Police Officers how to be United Nations Peacekeepers that I was forced to really learn the system. Part of their ten week training program included a really good block of instruction on land navigation. I was very comfortable teaching the map and compass portion but I was pretty shaky on the GPS. So prior to the class I spent several days reading the manual and using the GPS unit in every way imaginable until I developed a pretty good understanding of this tool and I was later successful at teaching hundreds of Nepalese how to use it. The training was pretty simple because I divided the operation of the GPS receiver into three different phases: Pre-Mission Setup, During Mission Use, and Post Mission Analysis. Before we get into how to use the receiver lets first identify what it can do well and what it cannot do at all.

How does a GPS work?

How the Global Positioning System works is not that complicated. All GPS receivers are a distance ranging system. This means that the only thing that the GPS is trying to do is determine how far it is from the satellites. The GPS satellites are a network of satellites that orbit the earth and send unique signals to GPS receivers on earth providing the device with precise details of the receiver's location, the time of day, and the speed the device is moving in relation to the satellite. The GPS operates on the principle of trilateration. Once a GPS receiver has distances for at least three satellites, it can perform the trilateration calculations. Trilateration works in a similar way to pinpointing your position on a map knowing the precise distance from three different landmarks using a back azimuth. Where the three azimuths overlap is your location.

What a GPS does well

The GPS can quickly identify your current location and elevation within a few meters/feet of error anywhere on earth

Once the GPS has been setup properly it will display its current location in Military Grid Reference System (MGRS) coordinates, latitude and longitude coordinates, and elevation in relation to sea level.

The GPS records its exact location in the "tracks" which can be downloaded to a computer

When the GPS is turned and connected to at least three satellites it is recording its location and that information is stored in memory until erased or recorded over by new data. These tracks as well as waypoints that are recorded can be downloaded to a computer and used for post mission analysis. These tracks and waypoints can also be overlaid on a map. I have found that important target data can be saved

Can give current time, time of sunrise and sunset

Once the GPS is properly set up it will give current time plus sunset and sunrise. These times are important when planning operations around darkness as well as tracking the position of the sun. The guerrilla sniper should always try to keep the sun to his back so his enemy has the sun in their eyes.

Can be used worldwide because it works off satellites and not cell phone towers

The GPS system is a global system so it can be used wherever there is a clear view of the sky.

It is a passive system that cannot be tracked

The handheld GPS unit mentioned in this article sends out no signal so it cannot be tracked. It is a receiver only, it transmits nothing. A phone on the other hand does send out signals and even though they can be enabled to give GPS coordinates they should be avoided.

What a GPS does not do well

The GPS is not a replacement for a handheld compass.

The compass feature on the GPS will work if you set the unit down and walk away for several minutes. Every time you move the unit the arrow is now pointed in the wrong direction until the unit corrects. Bottom line is the correction takes too long for it to be used for successful orienteering.

The GPS is not a replacement for a map

Most GPS units have a small map screen but unless you have downloaded detailed maps to the GPS unit the ones provided have little to no detail. Most likely the screen will show tracks and where you moved from but will give no details of the terrain features like roads, waterways, and hills. Even with detailed maps loaded into the GPS unit the screen size will be too small to orient the GPS's map to the terrain features seen with naked eye. There is no substitute for a large unfolded map for situational awareness. The GPS receiver can assist in locating your current location on that conventional paper map. The GPS receiver should be used in unison with a map, each enhancing the other.

The GPS is not good at navigating to unknown locations

Unless you already have the coordinates of the destination and can enter them into your GPS unit it will only track where you are or where you have been. If you do enter the coordinates into the GPS it will give straight line navigation with no accommodation for terrain.

The GPS is not good at navigating around obstacles that can hinder navigation

The GPS navigation features deals in straight line navigation. It will walk you off a cliff or through a lake if those terrain features are in between you and your destination. When the GPS and map are utilized together these terrain features can be avoided.

The GPS will not connect to satellites without a clear view of the sky

Because the GPS relies on satellites they don't work well inside of buildings. The roof material blocks the signal being transmitted by the GPS network satellite. I have also had problems at the bottom of steep canyons when there is limited view of the sky. An external antenna can be used but it does not come standard with most units and the external antennae must be placed outside. Another consideration with most external antennas is that their cords are only 10 feet long

GPS setup and use for the sniper

How to set up a new "out of the box" GPS receiver

Any new GPS is going to be set to factory default settings. These factory settings are of little use and need to be changed. The first and most important thing to change is the system notification; mute all the sounds.

SETUP – SYSTEM

Enable WAAS. Wide Area Augmentation System (WAAS) was developed by the Federal Aviation Administration (FAA) to increase the accuracy of the GPS system to aviation standards. It should be enabled in North America to benefit from the increase in accuracy, but outside that area will just drain the GPS receiver's battery more quickly.

SETUP – UNITS

- Select Military Grid Reference System (MGRS) if working with military maps otherwise use Latitude and Longitude.
- Select WGS 84 for the map datum unless your maps are something different.
- I choose the Metric system for distance, elevation, and speed. Or you can select another option. It really depends on what you are familiar with.

SETUP – TIME

- 24 hour
- My GPS is set for US Eastern time. Make sure it is set to your time and not the default.
- Daylight savings time – Auto

Maps

Unless you purchase maps with your GPS receiver it will not have any installed. I successfully downloaded maps for most of the world from www.gpsfiledepot.com and installed them on my GPS 60CSX. I had to add a 16 GB memory chip which gave me sufficient space to store all the maps of my area of operation. Because I cannot store every map I own I move and replace maps when I travel overseas. I keep all of mine stored on a laptop computer. To move the maps I connect the GPS receiver into the laptop via a USP cord. I use the Garmin software Mapsource that came with the GPS receiver. Garmin has a newer program called Basecamp that works in the same way. Whatever GPS, software, and computer you choose commit to using the programs and learning the system. Maps and data are like any intelligence gathering. It is about capturing and exploiting.

Customize the display option

The next part of the pre-mission setup is to customize each of the display options to bring all the relevant data to one page to minimize having to change pages and search for the data. Refer to the example below for the ideal front page setup.

When I am teaching someone in person how to do this I normally have them change all the displays and then I choose the factory default option so they have to go through the process again. Approximately four times is about what it takes to become really comfortable with the system. Repetition is the best way to learn the GPS. The idea here is to become an expert with whatever GPS you are using so the more time spent using it the better.

Time of Day	Accuracy
Sunrise	Sunset
Elevation	Speed
Location in Latitude and Longitude	
Location in MGRS	

Suggested GPS setup

Ideal setting compared to factory setting

Operational considerations for GPS usage

Pre-Mission

Make sure that you are outside with an unobstructed view of the sky. Let's work from the beginning as if we just took the brand new receiver out of the box. First familiarize yourself with the receiver by identifying the location of its buttons, the battery cover, and any covers for external plugs. The next step is to place good quality batteries in the unit and turn it on. Familiarize yourself with the start up, shut down, and back light features. It will take a few minutes for the receiver to connect to the satellites and begin to receive data. Familiarize yourself with the different screens and the data on each screen. The next step is to calibrate the GPS receiver so look for two very important icons: SETUP and UNITS.

Pre-mission checklist

- Check the batteries and spares
- Install the right maps for the mission
- Verify target waypoints if set
- Verify the settings and make sure the sound it turned OFF
- Attach dummy cord from GPS to pouch to prevent loss

Operational use of the GPS during the mission

Using the GPS during the mission is ideal during map checks. A map check is done during a security halt to verify route and current location. It is easy in the tactical environment to get lost, which can be deadly in a hostile environment. It is tempting when lost that we speed up instead of stopping to verify our location and then making the right correction.

Waypoints can be set for hiding equipment and places of interest that can later be downloaded to overlay a map. These places of interest can be valuable sources of intelligence.

During Mission Checklist

- Monitor battery usage
- Situational awareness: verify location and direction of travel
- Set additional waypoints necessary for future hides or for intelligence value
- Make sure GPS is secure in pouch and don't lose it

Post Mission

Check the unit for damage and record battery life. Keep the battery life in your mind for future missions so you know how many extra to bring. Write down any waypoints you saved in your notebook or record them on a map.

Post mission checklist

- Download tracks and any added waypoints
- Compare actual route to planned route for the After Action Review (AAR)
- Replace batteries

Operational Security Considerations

If you are using the GPS receiver operationally be careful of the information that it has saved. If you are captured there is incriminating information that can be downloaded and used to identify the guerrilla sniper. Just having a GPS when detained by the new government's forces may be enough to have you held for years as a forward observer or spy. Target data can be saved into the unit in the text area but be careful what you record. Also losing your GPS unit during an operation will ensure it gets into the wrong hands. Consider a dummy cord to prevent loss.

This page is intentionally left blank

Chapter 12

Guerrilla Sniper Training

The aim of military training is not to just prepare men for battle but to make them long for it.

Louis Simpson

Guerrilla Sniper Training

Training is what differentiates the warriors from everyone else. Training is essential to developing critical combat skills and then continuing to train to maintain those skills. If an untrained person wakes up one day and decides that they want to set off to the woods and become a guerrilla sniper and they have no military background or extensive firearms experience they will likely perish very quickly. As anyone who has fired a rifle knows marksmanship takes time, practice, and lots of practice ammunition. Having extra training ammunition may not be an option under a totalitarian state where firearms are banned. Another consideration is security. Nothing draws attention like gunfire and the last thing the guerrilla sniper wants is to draw the attention of the new government's forces because of training. Knowledge and experience cannot be taken away even if gun and equipment has to be abandoned. Training falls into two important categories: general sniper training and mission specific sniper training.

General sniper training

- Fitness
- Fundamentals of marksmanship
- Tactics
- Field craft

An important note about fitness

Proper fitness level is essential for the guerrilla sniper. There is no substitute for being able to run, jump, and climb without becoming fatigued. A fatigued person is less capable and makes poor decisions. A great example of a proper fitness level is being able to run 5 miles in less than an hour, do 50 pushups, and 50 sit-ups. Fitness has the advantage of not being "tactical" so the guerrilla sniper should be able to continue physical training regardless of the security situation. Cross-county running and hiking are a great way to reconnoiter areas while maintaining operational fitness levels.

Fundamentals of marksmanship

- Steady and stable shooting position
- Correct sight alignment/ correct sight picture
- Breath control
- Trigger control
- Follow through

The most important aspect of precision shooting is consistency. The same sight picture, trigger pull, etc can mean the difference between a controlled grouping of bullets or wildly missing the target. Take these fundamentals seriously and practice often. Marksmanship is a perishable skill.

Six factors of a good shooting position

- Muscle relaxation
- Bone support
- Natural point of aim (comfort test)
- Elbows under weapon
- Core muscle support instead of extremities muscle support
- Proper eye relief and relaxed neck

A good house is built on a firm foundation and so is a good shooting position. A firm foundation means bone support instead of muscle support because muscles get shaky when they are fatigued. Remember: a relaxed shooting position is a good shooting position. A great rule of thumb is to get as low to the ground as possible and use a pack for the best, most stable position.

What ranges should the guerrilla sniper train to shoot?

The advantage of the scoped precision rifle is that it is capable to hitting man sized targets far past what an assault rifle can expect to hit. When we define how far, it is really a matter of the caliber of the rifle. It is recommended that the guerrilla sniper choose a rifle that is at least a 308 caliber because anything smaller is affected by the wind too much and hitting targets past 500 yards becomes problematic. There are skilled snipers who can shoot the smaller calibers effectively but they would be the first to tell you that smaller calibers require more wind adjustment and greater skill. So the answer of how far to engage targets is no closer than 400 yards, out to about 800 yards, depending on the capability of the sniper but 600 yards is probably ideal. The precision rifle gives guerrilla sniper a "ballistic advantage" of the conventional forces armed with assault rifles. It is important to the survival of the guerrilla sniper to not engage close targets or to jump up and start running after firing because the human eye is drawn to sudden movement. A close quarters running gunfight with a bolt action precision rifle must be avoided.

Train to shoot a specific part of the target

By training to shoot a specific place on the target, the shooter greatly increases his accuracy and likelihood of a hit.

Take training seriously

As an instructor if I have to choose between talented student and committed student I will choose commitment. I know that someone who is passionate about shooting will spend the time needed to master the fundamentals and appreciate the skills they have worked hard to achieve.

Field craft

Operating in a hostile environment requires specific tactical and survival skills. These skills include camouflage, land navigation, and understanding the difference between cover and concealment. By using the terrain and its features to mask ground movement the guerrilla sniper can remain hidden from hostile forces. Further field craft skills include obstacle crossing, selecting good firing positions, constructing a final firing up position, effective observation, and target selection. In the hostile environment counter surveillance, detecting the enemy, and target selection are critical skills. Good field craft also includes survival, evasion, and escape techniques. The best way to train in field craft is to spend considerable time and effort in a simulated combat environment. Often times hunting of elusive and dangerous game is an excellent training opportunity to further develop field craft skills.

The guerrilla sniper should practice the following shooting positions

- Prone supported (use the bipod or backpack for a rock solid rest)
- Prone unsupported (keep elbows under the rifle and use sling for additional support)
- Kneeling (bone support by placing elbows on the knee and use sling for additional support)
- Sitting (more stable than kneeling but slower to recover from)
- Standing (keep the elbows in and use core muscles or use a tree for stability)

Mission specific training and preparation

Once a specific mission plan is chosen it is time to prepare for that mission. Training prior to each mission, even just conducting a simple rehearsal, greatly increases the likelihood of success. How much time is allowed for pre mission training depends on the complexity of the mission and how much time is available. A fairly simple mission like an assassination may only require minimal training like zeroing the rifle for the range the sniper is planning on shooting from. For this example the mission plan is to hide in a specific area 600 yards away from the target. So the sniper would zero the rifle for 600 yards prior to the mission and work on the fundamentals of marksmanship by shooting at that range in similar conditions as the actual mission. Once the assassination mission is complete the guerrilla sniper would then change the zero back to the setting previous to the mission.

The Guerrilla Sniper Tactics Handbook

Chapter 13

Conducting Guerrilla Sniper Operations

Never was anything great achieved without danger

Niccolo Machiavelli

Conducting Guerrilla Sniper Operations

The operation and firing cycle

- Gather available Intelligence
- Conduct reconnaissance (maps, photographs, surveillance)
- Movement
    - Get close to release point quickly non tactical
    - Release point (transition into tactical movement)
    - Use rally points as fall back points and security halts
    - Objective rally point. The last rally point before the objective. Time to drop non essential gear and finalize camouflage.
- Maneuver to Primary Final Firing Position (FFP) or Alternate FFP
- Retreat to fall back position if FFP compromised
- Return to Objective Rally point after firing and consolidate equipment
- Return home/back to friendly area by different route
- Conduct after action review (AAR)
- Analyze and integrate intelligence for future missions

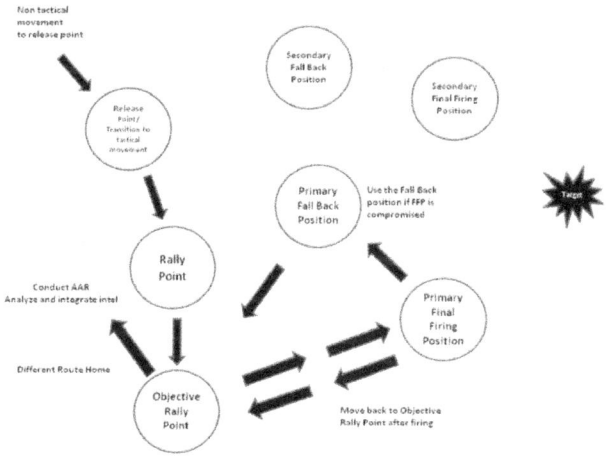

The operation and firing cycle model

The acronym METTTCM is the driving force behind all tactical planning.

- Mission - What is the intended mission? Who, what, when, why, and how should be explained?
- Enemy - Who is the enemy, what is their mission, how are they equipped, how will they react?
- Terrain and weather - What is the terrain in the area and what will the weather be like during the mission?

- Troops - What are the friendly troops that are available to complete the mission?
- Support available - What support is available to the forces completing the mission?
- Time available - When does this mission need to be completed?
- Civil considerations - Are there civilians in the area and how will they react to this mission?
- Media considerations - How will the media react to this mission? What can be said about it?

Use the acronym OCOKA to see terrain through strategic eyes

- Observation and Fields of Fire –Identify potential engagement areas, defensible terrain, where to place weapon systems, and identify where maneuvering forces are most vulnerable.
- Cover and Concealment – Cover are things that will stop bullets. Concealment is something natural or man-made that can be used to conceal, hide, or camouflage.
- Obstacles (man-made and natural) – Any natural or man-made terrain that stops, impedes, slows, or diverts movement.

- Key or Decisive Terrain – Some terrain features which if controlled will give a marked advantage to whoever controls it.
- Avenues of Approach – Is any air or ground route that can be used to lead to the objective or to the key terrain features.

Types of firing positions for the guerrilla sniper

- Primary FFP - The firing position that gives shooter the best view of the target area, the best concealment, and the best escape routes. The primary FFP is considered the best firing point.
- Alternate FFP -The alternate firing position used in the event that for some reason the primary FFP is no longer available usually because of changes in the tactical environment.
- Fallback position - A position that is pre-determined to be where the shooter goes after engaging targets and drawing the attention of the new government's forces. The position should give some view of the target area as well as the primary FFP. Firing from the fallback position should only be in self defense and should be avoided.

- Belly scratch hides – Is a temporary shooting position which is the length, width, and depth of one person. This is ideal because it is quick, temporary, and offers good protection.

The final firing position (FFP) tactical considerations

- Use a belly scratch hide for hasty rural hides. Don't build permanent hides or fill sandbags.
- Rely on natural cover and concealment.
- Protect against drones, thermal detection, and electronic surveillance.
- When the FFP is abandoned sanitize it like it is a crime scene: Leave no fingerprints DNA, brass, food, etc.
- Consider the back of rooms, attic space, and loopholes in urban environment.
- Choose the position that allows you to control the area with the narrowest field of view.
- Always plan for more than one alternate FFPs and fallback positions in case the primary are blocked or become less ideal. Primary, secondary, tertiary...etc.

Nice tools to have to construct the hide

- Gloves to protect hands and conceal fingerprints
- Screen to be placed in front of the sniper for concealment
- Drill or chisel to make loop holes
- Pry bar to make loop holes and open locked doors
- Lock pick to open locked doors clandestinely
- Parachute cord, zip ties, and tape for modifications to the FFP
- Folding chair or table for room hides

Tactics specific to the guerrilla sniper

The world of the guerrilla sniper is a war of nerves, concentration, and endurance. Be meticulous about gathering intelligence. Do not fire until you are absolutely certain of a kill. If you fire and miss you reveal your own position. Where, when, and under what circumstances are the new government's forces operating in the area? Analyze the enemy and then reconnoiter the ground and work out how the enemy is operating. Aim to be completely invisible, even to the trained eye. Create distractions, wear them down with diversionary movements, and exhaust their ability to fight you by remaining hidden. Remember that everything depends upon exhaustive intelligence, meticulous preparation, careful attention to detail, and endless patience.

Additional guerrilla sniper tactics

- Have the ability to blend in with the locals
- FFPs should be low to the ground; setting up on a hill or in tower is too obvious.
- Put the sun behind you.
- The human eye is naturally drawn to sudden movement.
- There are snipers hunting you.
- If you shoot more than two rounds from a single location you are likely to get flanked by infantry, captured, and killed.
- Remember you have a sniper rifle. **DON'T GET TOO CLOSE** Use the ballistic advantage of your rifle.
- The guerrilla sniper should have the ability to shed everything tactical in the event that the sniper is picked up by the new government's forces. If they have no evidence they will likely release the guerrilla after being held for a few days.

- Trust your instincts – Fear is your friend, don't suppress your natural fear, instead use it like a sixth sense. Find the source of the danger and trust yourself.
- Always value common sense. If it does not sound right or look right then avoid it.

Pre Combat Checks (PCC)

A pre combat check is an inspection done ideally within two hours of conducting the operation. The emphasis of the inspection is to verify that all mission essential equipment is accounted for and pre positioned for easy access. All weapons should be checked to include magazines loaded. Any equipment that is found to be missing or deficient should be located or repaired. The PCC is essential to mission success. Not conducting PCC is a guarantee the mission essential equipment will be forgotten.

This page is intentionally left blank

Chapter 14

After Action Reviews and Intelligence Gathering for Future Operations

If you want a picture of the future, imagine a boot stamping on a human face –

forever.

George Orwell 1984

After Action Reviews and Intelligence Gathering for Future Operations

After you have conducted your first successful mission it is tempting to pat yourself on the back a little too much. The mission is not over until the after action review is conducted and the intelligence is analyzed and integrated into future operations.

The After Action Review (AAR)

An essential part of self improvement is the ability to take a step back from yourself and give an honest account of performance. There is nothing wrong with mistakes when they are identified, learned from, and corrected. There is no such thing as a perfect operation; there is always room for improvement. The best way to conduct this post mission analysis is to conduct either a formal or informal after action review.

The Formal AAR

The formal AAR is designed for groups where one person both conducts and takes notes. It is important to mention that the AAR is not a bitch session where the members become defensive; it is a professional development tool. It is usually best that the commander or leader of a mission not be the one who conduct the AAR because often times they will see criticism as a slight on their planning, leadership, and execution. The person conducting has the responsibility to keep the AAR on track and professional. It is best to remind all the participants that the purpose is not to make anyone person look good or bad but to give an honest evaluation of the facts.

For the formal AAR these questions should be posed to all the participants in the mission

- What was supposed to happen?
- What did happen?
- What are some improvements?
- What are some things to keep the same next time?
- What can be done to improve the training next time?

The informal AAR

The informal AAR is for individual to evaluate their own actions. The guerrilla sniper regardless of whether he participated in a group operation or as a lone wolf should conduct an informal AAR evaluating his own performance. Honesty and humility go a long way towards self improvement. Making 20 mistakes on the first mission and 10 mistakes on the second mission is improvement. Identifying that you are untrained and then seeking out training to correct the lack of knowledge is a warrior's responsibility.

Three basic questions for the informal AAR

- What did I do right?
- What did I do wrong?
- What should I do differently next time?

Analyze and integrate intelligence

The guerrilla sniper should always be seeking knowledge, intelligence, and self improvement. There are multiple ways to get intelligence using overt and covert methods. Remember that intelligence that is not captured and exploited is intelligence that is wasted. The lessons learned, the sacrifices made, and targets engaged are critical intelligence for future operations.

List of intelligence gathering sources

Operational intelligence

- Intelligence gathered directly from the battlefield
- Analyze enemy tactics, techniques, procedures
- Intelligence taken from deceased combatants

Human intelligence

- Paid informants
- Sympathetic civilians
- Patrolling
- POWs or detainees
- Refugees
- Travelers
- Cab drivers

Geospatial intelligence

- Satellite imagery

- Aerial photography
- Maps
- Terrain data

Open source intelligence

- Internet
- General military and technical manuals
- Books and magazines
- Social media

Signals intelligence

- Scanner to intercept non encrypted communication

Technical intelligence

- Gathered by the analysis of weapons and equipment

Chapter 15

Mission Planning and Preparation

Benefits should be conferred gradually; and in that way they will taste better.

Niccolo Machiavelli

Mission Planning and Preparation for the Tactical Team

There is no greater tool for the scout sniper team than the mission planning and preparation process. The old adage of failing to plan is paramount to planning to fail it true. Use these important steps to plan out ht missions using every available mean at your disposal. Use the 1/3 2/3 rule for mission planning and execution. That rule being 1/3 of the allotted time should be for planning and 2/3 of the allotted time should be left for preparation and execution.

There are two classifications of operations that snipers participate in for planning purposes.

- Immediate actions
- Deliberate actions

Immediate actions are ones that require snipers to react to a critical situation with little or no planning because the more time thinking about "what to do" or "how to do it" translate to innocent lives lost. Snipers arrive at an incident and follow either an SOP (standard operating procedure) or use their best judgment based on experience and training to quickly resolve the crisis and most importantly save lives.

Deliberate actions are ones were the situation does not require urgency. There is time to plan and compare courses of action, request additional personnel and equipment as required, and only begin the operation after planning and asset organization is complete. Typically these types of deliberate action operations are more flexible on when they need to be completed and when they must begin.

Mission planning Considerations

By adapting the US Military mission planning and operations order we can develop a template for operational planning that ensures missions are planned completely, understood by those carrying it out, and presented in the most professional manner possible. It is imperative that every team member understands the commander's intent, have an overall concept of the operation, and collectively be able to complete the mission even if they are given no additional guidance. The reason for developing a template for operational planning is so that missions are planned completely but not to encourage planning to become complicated or elaborate. Mission plans should be as simple as the mission will allow because it has been proven through training and real world operations that simple tactical plans have a higher likelihood its success because there is less moving parts.

Eight step Troop Leading Procedure

1. Receive the mission
2. Issue a warning order
3. Make a tentative plan
4. Initiate movement
5. Conduct Reconnaissance
6. Complete the plan
7. Issue the operations order
8. Supervise and refine

Mission planning: The outline of the entire process.

1. Receive mission

2. Issue the warning order and coordinate with other team leaders (scouts, snipers, breachers, assaulters, medics)

3. Make a tentative plan based on mission planning template

a. Make a tentative plan based on:

METT-TCM

- Mission
- Enemy
- Terrain and weather
- Troops and support available
- Time available
- Civil considerations
- Media: political and public image considerations

OAKOC

- Observation and fields of fire
- Avenues of approach
- Key and decisive terrain
- Obstacles
- Cover and concealment

   b. Analyze courses of action

   c. Compare courses of action

e. Decision

4. Initiate movement

5. Reconnaissance to confirm finalized plan

6. Complete the plan and coordinate with other assets

7. Issue the operations order and rehearse

8. Supervise and refine

Operations Order Template

Paragraph <u>one</u>   **Situation**

1. Suspects (names, pictures, vehicle, family, criminal history)

2. Friendly (witnesses, informants, location of people not involved)

3. Other assets assisting the operation not normally assigned

Paragraph <u>two</u> **Mission**

1. A clear and concise statement expressed in the; who, what, when, were, and why.

Paragraph <u>three</u> **Execution**

1. Concept of the operation (Leaders visualization of the operation from start to finish. Accurately describes the commander's intent so the mission can be accomplished in the event of no further instruction.)

    a. movement and actions at the objective

    b. location of people and equipment during the operation

    c. mission of attached/ assisting officers and agencies.

Paragraph <u>four</u> **Service/ Support**

1. Paramedics, fire department, Power Company, Gas Company, and other assisting agencies

2. Nearest trauma 1 hospital and best route

3. Medical helicopter support and landing zone designation with grid coordinates

Paragraph <u>five</u> **Command and Signal**

1. Incident commander

2. Chain of command

3. Communications

- radio frequencies
- Individual call numbers

This page intentionally left blank

Chapter 16

Fundamentals of Man Tracking

We have forty million reasons for failure but not a single excuse.

Rudyard Kipling

Fundamentals of Man Tracking

The Guerrilla/Sniper should understand the fundamental aspects of human tracking. These fundamentals, combined with a great deal of practice, will enable the Scout/Sniper to track a human or group of humans with reasonable accuracy. Also by having the ability to track others the Sniper will be able to better conceal his tracks to prevent detection, capture, and death.

Tracking is the ability to follow the movements and determine the activities of men and animals through the signs left behind by their movement. A sign is any visible disturbance of the natural environment caused by the movement of humans or animals. A track is the path used by men or animals, and is formed by connecting a series of signs together in chronological order. To the vast majority of contemporary humanity, tracking humans or animals is a lost art. For Scout/Snipers, tracking must be an essential skill, one that will best allow Scout/Snipers to fulfill their primary mission to maintain contact with the enemy. Tracking is often a very efficient method for locating the enemy. Without it, Scout/Snipers will spend a great deal of time reconnoitering large areas until the enemy is seen or heard. In many environments, this method will yield few positive results. Conversely, knowing how to track will also enable Scout/Snipers to take measures which will make it much more difficult for the enemy to track them, clearly an equally important skill. Tracking is a skill which requires much experience and practice to master. To succeed in tracking, a Scout/Sniper must be very familiar and aware of the natural environment. It is difficult to detect signs (a visible disturbance of the natural environment), when one does not know how the natural environment should look. This instruction is designed to provide the Scout/Sniper with the basics of tracking and with enough knowledge to begin learning how to track in the field. Again, only much experience and practice will enable a Scout/Sniper to gain any degree of proficiency in this art.

Sign

A tracker is totally dependent on sign to find the enemy. Every man and animal leaves some sort of sign when moving through a natural environment (and sometimes even in an urban environment.) An expert tracker will usually be able to find sign, and thus his quarry, under all but impossible conditions. This paragraph will outline the basic types of sign to look for when tracking the enemy.

Examples of Sign

- Footprints or portions of footprints
- Direction of grass, leaves, and sticks kicked up by the feet
- Unnatural formation of vines, grass and plants
- Sap exuding from cuts and bruises on roots
- Change in color of foliage
- Dirt smudges on rocks, logs and leaves
- Broken cobwebs up to a man's height
- Moss scraped from trees and rocks
- Disturbance of animal and insect life
- Disturbance to water where people have climbed out or stepped in to streams or puddles
- Stones and rocks removed from their original position
- Broken twigs and shoots
- Blood stains

Places Where It Is Easy To Locate Sign

- These places are easy to located signs left behind by the enemy, so more attention should be given in these areas. The enemy will find it rather difficult to conceal their signs in these areas.
- Along river banks/streams.
- In places where the grass and undergrowth is thick.
- Places where the slopes are steep.
- Newly tilled land.
- Logs and dead tress lying across streams, rivers or ravines.
- Places Difficult For Tracking

These places are rather difficult to locate enemy signs, thus making tracking difficult

- Along well used track, hardened tracks, and roads
- Along big rivers
- In villages or inhabited areas
- Area of operation of friendly forces
- Artillery and mortar impact areas
- Signs Found In Various Conditions

- Secondary Jungle, Woods, Grassy Areas
- Change in color of foliage.
- Breaking of shoots and twigs.
- Lanes created in direction of movement.
- Footprints or portions of footprints on soft ground.
- Broken cobwebs up to a man's height.
- Breaking or bending of small plants.
- Disturbance to insects and animal life.
- Particles of sand, mud and soil left behind.

Rocky Areas

The common signs found in these areas.

- Small stones moved from their original positions.
- Moss on stones which have been stepped upon.
- Scratches on stones made by boots, weapons or packs.
- Footprints or portions of footprints on rocks.
- Mud and soil left behind from sole of boots.

Along Streams

The common signs found along streams.

- Disturbance of water.
- Footprints at river banks and on rocks.
- Signs on logs, roots and tress lying across rivers.
- Disturbance to vegetation along river banks.
- Sign On The Ground. Signs on the ground are signs which are found not above 6 inches from the ground. The common signs on the ground are:
- Footprints or portion of footprints
- Slanted fens and grasses
- Scratches on rocks and logs
- Stones being removed from their original position
- Disturbance to animal and insects life
- Scratched roots
- Sand and mud dropped from soles of boots
- Rubbish that was left behind
- Broken dead twigs and dead leaves
- Signs Above The Ground

- Signs above the ground are all signs that are found above 6 inches from the ground to man's height. The common signs above the ground are:
- Bending/slanting of small plants
- Change in color of foliage
- Breaking of spider webs
- Mud on sole of boots smeared onto tree trunks and leaves
- Scratches on bark of trees, branches and rocks
- Broken twigs

Information Obtained From Sign

The following information can be obtained by careful reading and assessment of signs made by the enemy:

- Direction of track
- Age of tracks or signs
- Number of enemy
- Type and approximate weight of equipment carried
- Sex of enemy
- Speed of movement
- Type of food being eaten

- Enemy intentions
- Enemy tactics
- Wounded enemy

Factors Which Make Tracking Difficult

These factors will affect our ability to track successfully.

- Darkness. Only dogs can track at night
- Strong winds
- Weather conditions
- Time limitations and mission requirements

Reading Sign

Sign On Enemy Tracks/Trails

When a human being moves from one place to another, he will leave behind signs which will be very valuable to a tracker. The enemy may camouflage his signs to avoid being detected. Nevertheless, he is bound to leave behind some signs accidentally, which will assist the tracker in tracking them. Some common signs usually found on track are:

- Footprints or portions of footprints

- Signs left behind on soft ground
- Small plants and grasses stepped upon
- Roots that are scratched
- Booby trap markings
- Excess food, cigarette butts, match sticks, and other equipment accidentally dropped or left behind.
- Signs of enemy deceptions and camouflage
- Signs at track junctions

Sign at Enemy Temporary Resting Places

Signs commonly found in enemy temporary resting place are:

- Signs where enemy sat down to rest, such as footprints.
- Signs of enemy leaning onto tree trunks and rocks.
- Sentry positions.
- Broken dray twigs and leaves at resting places.
- Signs of weapons left on the ground, especially the support weapons.
- Food droppings, cigarette butts, match sticks, etc.
- Signs of entry and exit into resting places.

Sign in Permanent or Semi-Permanent Camps

- Trenches and shelters
- Water points
- Latrines
- Cooking areas and fire places
- Cut wood and wood splinters
- Communications wires and alarm systems
- Sentry posts/observations posts
- Booby traps
- Routes in and out of camps

Sign at Enemy Water Points

The enemy is very careful when selecting a water point. Their water point is usually located in an area where they are difficult to be located. These places are usually in difficult terrain and on small streams. Common signs that indicate the presence of a water point are:

- Signs of ground being dug and stones arranged to deepen the water
- Use of bamboo to channel water from water point to base, etc
- Signs of soap and bathing areas
- Sentry posts

- Routes in and out

Sign In Ambush Positions.

Signs that are commonly found in an abandoned ambush position are:

- Changes in the natural environment
- Signs of ambush groups, such as killer groups, sentries and cut offs
- Firm base or resting place
- Signs of booby traps
- Broken twigs and leaves
- Communication wire and old camouflage

How to Analyze the Enemy

The ability of a combat tracker to analyze signs is very important in finding the enemy. Some of the information that can be obtained is:

- Enemy Strength
- Enemy activities
- Weapons, food, and other equipment
- Speed and direction of movement
- Is anyone wounded?

Enemy Strength

To determine enemy strength we can consider the following:

- Footprints or portions of footprints on tracks/trails
- Signs in enemy resting places
- Signs in permanent and temporary camps
- Signs in ambush position
- Information from intelligence sources

Analyzing Footprints

Footprints may indicate direction and rate of movement, number of persons in the moving party, whether or not heavy loads are being carried, sex of members of the party, and whether the members of the party know they are being followed. Deep footprints with a long stride indicate running. Prints can be counted to determine numbers. If the prints are deep, short, and widely spaced, with indications of scuffing or shuffling, a heavy load is being carried by the person who left the print. The sex of the person being followed can be determined by studying the size and position of the footprints. Women generally tend to be pigeon-toed, while men usually walk with their feet straight ahead or pointed slightly to the outside. Women's prints are smaller and the stride is shorter than a man's. If the party realizes that they are being followed, an attempt to hide their tracks may be made. Persons walking backward have a short, irregular stride. The prints have an unusually deep toe. Soil will be kicked in the direction of movement. Pivots marks will show the enemy is checking to his rear. Since the last man in a file will normally leave the clearest footprints, his will be the key set of prints. A stick can be cut to match the length of the key print and notched to indicate width at the widest part of the sole. The tracker should compare the angle of the print to the direction of travel to determine how the person walks. Also he should look for identifying mark or feature on the print, such as a worn or frayed part of footwear, to help him identify the key print. In case the trail becomes vague or obliterated, or the trail being followed merges with another, the tracker can use his stick measuring device and close study to identify the key print. This will help him stay on the trail of the group being followed. The box method can be used to count up to 18 sets of track on the trail. There are two ways the tracker can employ the box method.

The first and most accurate is to use the stride as a unit of measure. This is used when a key print can be determined. By identifying the key print on a trail and drawing a line from the heel of the foot across the trail or road, then moving forward to the opposite print made by the same person and drawing a line through the instep, the tracker forms a box with the edges of the road or trail forming the sides and the lines he has drawn as the front and back. The tracker then counts every print inside the box to determine the number of person. Any person walking normally would have stepped in the box at least one time. The key print should be counted as one. The second way a tracker may use the box method is the 36-inch box. The tracker marks off a 36-inch cross section of the trail, counts the prints or indentations in the box, then divides the two to determine the number of persons that used the trail (The M16 rifle is 35 inches long and may be used as a measuring device.) By simply knowing the length of equipment makes a great reference.

Enemy Activities

To accurately determine enemy activities, a great amount of intelligence work is required. However some of the factors that can be found by the tracker teams are:

- Signs of enemy patrols/patrolling
- Signs of enemy hunting for food
- Signs of enemy contacting their supporter or other units
- Signs of enemy ambushes
- Signs of enemy caches

Enemy Equipment

Some of the aids that will reveal to us the equipment used by the enemy are:

- Old or torn clothing left behind or dropped
- Used ammunition casings that were dropped or left behind
- Wrappings of field dressing/bandages etc
- Wrappings of food and excess food left behind
- Support weapons prints on the ground
- Parts of booby traps and booby trap making equipment

Speed of Movement

The speed of movement depends on the tactics and techniques used by the enemy. A big group of enemy will take a longer time to move compared to a small group of enemy. As a guide to determine the speed of movement of the enemy we can consider the following:

Fast Movement or Under Pressure

Footprints are clear and very little or no camouflage is done. A lot of top signs such as broken twigs, scratches on bark of trees and rocks are common.

Slow Movement

Very little or no signs are left behind. Maximize the use of deception and camouflage.

Enemy Gender

To determine the enemy gender we can consider the following:

- Foot and boot prints. Women tend to have smaller prints
- Clothing and other equipments that were dropped or left behind

Wounds

Bloodstains often will be in the form of drops left by the wounded person being followed. Blood indicators are not always on the ground. Blood can be smeared on leaves or twigs from a man's height to the ground. Determining the location of the wound on the man being followed can be made by studying the bloodstains. If the blood seems to be dripping steadily, it probably came from a wound on the trunk. If it appears to be scattered to the front, rear, or sides, the wound is probably on an extremity. Arterial wounds will appear to pour the blood at regular intervals, as if it were poured from a pitcher. If the wound is venous, the blood will pour steadily. A wound in the lung will deposit bloodstains that are pink, bubbly, and frothy. A bloodstain deposited from a head wound will appear heavy, wet, and slimy, like gelatin. Abdominal wounds often mix blood with digestive juices so that the deposit will have an odor, and the stains will be light in color. By studying the bloodstains, left by the wounded person, the tracker can determine the seriousness of the wound and estimate how far a person with this type of wound could move unassisted. This process should lead the tracker to enemy bodies or further indications as to where they have been carried.

Information Required by Trackers

Although a Scout/Sniper Team may chance upon sign left by the enemy, it is always best to begin in an area where enemy contact was made. The following information should be provided to the team in order to make tracking as easy as possible:

- Location and time of the last contact
- Type of contact
- Estimated enemy strength
- Type of uniforms and equipment used
- Direction of withdrawal
- Enemy casualties
- Civilian population and activities in the area

- Friendly units and activities in the area

Judging the Age of Sign

One of the most important aids to the correct interpretation of sign is being able to accurately judge when the sign was made. Judging the age of a sign is probably the most difficult part of tracking. Much experience and a thorough understanding of the environment are needed for this task. The first step in judging age is to fix the sign into a restricted time bracket. Obviously, the time that the sign was found is the latest time that the sign could have been made. To determine the actual age of the sign, consider the following.

Rain

Recall when it last rained. If the rain was light and the signs are pock marked, it indicates that the signs have been made before the rain. If the rain is heavy it will wash away all the sign and therefore the signs found are made after the rain.

Example: If a sign is found at 1200 hrs and there was a heavy rain at 0300 hrs and the sign is clear, it must have been made after the rain. We can therefore place it in a 9 hour time bracket. To narrow down on the time bracket a further study of the other factors must be made.

Mud

The state of dryness of a sign in mud or soft ground must be noted. If the sign is very fresh, water will not have run back into the depression made by the boot. Later, water runs back, and later still the mud which has been pushed up around the depression and kicked forward by the foot leaving the ground begins to dry, and impurities in the water begins to settle.

Animal Tracks Superimposed

Most animal lie up during the day and move at night. If human prints have animal tracks superimposed, and these tracks show that the animals have moved in both directions, the human prints are at least one night old. If the tracks show that the animals have moved only in one direction, then the human tracks have been made during the night after the animals have moved down to water points. You should study animal behavior first before you can consider animal prints in determining the age of the signs.

Sap

Most plants exude sap when cut or bruised. This is clearly visible when the roots are stepped upon. However, different types of sap dray and harden at different rates. To judge the age of sap, one needs to have local knowledge and experience.

Cracks and Bent Grass or Leaves

An indication of the age of a track may be gained by the dryness of such cracks. When fresh they are green, but after a few days turn brown; however, the amount of sunlight in the previous day must be considered. We must also consider that some leaves will dray faster than other leaves after being cut or broken.

Leaves Covering Track

In the forest, leaves are always falling down from the tress. The number of leaves depends on the season and the amount of wind and rain during the past few days. This will further indicate the age of tracks.

Fire

Fire is one of the best aids to judging age. Study the ashes, embers, and the plants surrounding the fire place.

Ants and Insects

A column of ants on the move usually moves in a single file, and if disturbed it will disperse. It will usually take 8-18 minutes for them to regroup. Spiders take about an hour to rebuild their web, usually in the evening.

Comparison Method

This is one of the best methods of judging age and can be employed as follows.

Footprints

Make another footprint alongside the track and compare the difference.

Vegetation

Break a branch of the same type of tree, grass of leaf, and compare the difference. All methods mentioned are used to assist in judging the age of tracks and sign. These all rely heavily on local knowledge and experience. They will act as a guide to an inexperienced tracker. Constant practice is required to be successful in judging age. Different environments will weather signs differently and at different rates. Wet climates will weather signs much faster than drier climates. The best method for judging the effects of the environment on aging signs is to conduct a test over several days to a week. In the test the tracker will establish a test trail using signs which he believes he will see in actual tracking operations. For instance, in the test trail the tracker will make some distinct footprints, will drop cigarette butts, cut various types of vegetation, enter and exit streams, drop brass cartridges and other metal debris, make a fire, bend twigs, trample grass, and make a bivouac site. Each day for a week, the tracker will carefully examine each sign and will note the subtle differences which have occurred in the sign. These differences will be carefully noted in a log book for future reference. Along with the changes in the condition of the sign, the tracker will also note environmental factors which occurred during each 24 hour period. This could be rain, dew, or strong wind. Once recorded and studied, these notes will be very helpful in determining the age of signs through their condition.

Tracking Techniques

The easiest method to track is to follow signs from one to another so as to literally walk in the same track as the enemy. Although this is the fastest and easiest method to track the enemy, it is also the most dangerous. The enemy may choose to booby trap his trail or to ambush any trackers following along the track. The scallop method may be used to increase the safety of the Scout/Sniper Team when following the enemy. In this technique, the trackers will find the track, follow it a short distance to determine the direction of movement, and then leave the trail to move around and ahead in an arc in order to pick up the trail further ahead. The size of the arc will depend on the terrain and vegetation. The scallop method will help the team avoid booby traps, and may foil stay-behind ambushes.

The following items should be kept in mind while tracking

- Observe as far forward of you as you can.
- Observe to locate directions of sign. (movement)
- Observe and locate the furthest sign.
- Always remember the direction you took by occasionally looking backwards.
- Be careful whenever there are more than one sign, especially at track junctions.
- Move tactically.
- Remember the distance you have taken and your location.
- Do not bluff yourself by imagining signs.
- Stop tracking when you are tired.
- Do not make any noise and observe the highest standard of field craft.
- Do not leave behind too many signs such as breaking or cutting twigs.
- Do not always observe the ground immediately forward of you.

Re-acquiring the Track

There will always be occasions when the tracker will fail to locate the next sign along a trail and then lose the track. When this situation occurs, the tracker must conduct a search drill.

There are four types of search drills to re-acquire the track:

- **Private Search**

    This is the first method used whenever a sign is lost. The tracker should mark the last confirmed sign, stop the rest of the team, and move forward about five paces looking for the next sign. If the tracker fails to locate the next sign, he should return to the last sign, and conduct a team search.

- **Round Search**

    The tracker, along with another Marine, should walk in a circle about 15-20 paces in diameter from the last confirmed sign, trying to locate the next sign.

- **Box Search**

    Like a round search, but the search patter is a square.

- **Cross Grain Search**

    In this method, the tracker and another Marine will move from the last conferment sign to a point 15-20 paces away, and then back again, slowly covering every foot of the circle or box they are searching.

Tips

- Do not move more than five paces from the last confirmed sign.
- Do not split from the team.
- Do not bluff yourself by imagining signs.
- Do fail to finish the search drill whenever you have located the sign because the enemy might have done a deception.

Tracking Dogs

Tracking dogs are a specialized form of hunting dog. A tracking dog must be teamed with a competent handler. A good tracker combined with a tracking dog and handler will make a formidable team. While a tracker works mainly from visual sign, the tracking dog follows the scent of man and of damaged vegetation. Dogs can track much faster than men. Of great significance is that dogs, unlike man, can track at night. A well-trained tracking dog will not bark, and will avoid baits, cover odors, or other materials used to throw the dog off the track. The dog does have some drawbacks, however. The dog will become tired after several hours of tracking, making it much less effective. The dog cannot differentiate between the scent of friendly forces and enemy forces. The dog provides no real security to the team, i.e. the dog usually will not indicate when it comes very near the quarry. Dogs will find it difficult to track in sandy or swampy areas. Lastly, strong winds, heavy rain, and hot sun will all rapidly dissipate the scent of the quarry.

Deception

A deception in tracking is any action taken by the enemy to purposely deceive a tracker. Deceptions can be used as a precautionary measure, in case the enemy might be followed, or may be taken if the enemy <u>knows</u> he is being followed. Most deceptions will not fool an expert tracker for very long. In and of themselves, deceptions can tell the tracker something about the enemy; at least he is sophisticated enough to use deceptive measures.

Walking Backwards

This is done mainly on soft ground or dusty patches. The mud flakes are kicked up by the heel instead of the toe. The heel marks tend to be deeper and the pace is shorter. Remember, no matter which way the footprints face, the movement of the legs always drag or push soil and vegetation in the direction of movement.

Walking in Streams or Stream Beds

This deception is to confuse the tracker on the direction of movement. The enemy might move upstream or downstream. A close inspection of the river bottom may reveal sufficient information. Signs of this deception include moss scraped off of rocks, mud in the water, foot marks on sand or stones, and logs lying across streams. The change in the color of overturned stones will all help show the direction the enemy has taken. Attention should also be paid to overhanging branches and vines, in case the enemy pulls himself up on them to leave the water. It is advisable to search both directions of the river before continuing the tracking.

Walking on the Edges of Paths

The enemy walks along the edges of foot paths, jumping from left to right of the track to confuse the tracker on the number of enemy.

Stepping into One Another's Steps

This is also another deception to disguise the number of enemy.

Splitting Into Small Groups

Follow the track with the most signs.

Dead End

Dead Ends may appear near the base or top of steep ridges or cliffs. Check the trees in the area for signs of climbing. Check the area around the dead end very carefully, to see if there are any underground entrances at the site. At cliffs, look for signs that the enemy used ropes to enable them to climb or descend the cliff.

Tip-Toeing

This is done mainly on soft ground or dusty patches. The toe of the boot will leave a much deeper impression than the heel, and the pace will be very short.

Enlarging the Track

The Enemy may purposely enlarge a track to lure a tracker into following it. This may be done to throw the tracker off of the main trail, or may be used to lure the tracker into the ambush or booby trapped area.

Walking Along Fallen Trees or Along Rocks

Check logs and rocks for staining, damage, or displacement.

Disguising the Soles of Boots

The enemy may wrap rags around his boots to disguise his track, and make it more difficult to determine information from this sign. A sophisticated enemy may carve wooden animal hooves to attach to their boot soles, or use a similar boot to the friendly forces to confuse trackers. The enemy may use women and children to cover their trail by having them walk behind them.

Reversing Signs

Combined with walking backward, the enemy may brush vegetation and twigs backward, to further simulate forward motion.

Crawling

The enemy may crawl along game trails to simulate the signs of small animals, and may leave minimal or no high signs.

Deception Summary

All these deceptions will delay a tracker, but the tracker must remember that the enemy does not have wings. Unless carried out by an expert, all forms of deception will often serve only to give a clearer indication of where the track is.

A careful search of the immediate vicinity will show what the type of deceptions that have been used. The tracker can then take the necessary action to overcome them and continue tracking.

Actions on Locating the Enemy

If a team is successful in tracking the enemy, they will eventually find him. Great care must be taken when the enemy is near or when very fresh tracks have been found. Great care should be taken when following fresh tracks. Trackers should be very alert for all signs of the enemy when fresh tracks are discovered. Typical signs include noise made by the enemy, movement of any sort, and alarmed birds or insects. Don't follow someone with no plan what to do when found.

Counter tracking

There are few expert trackers in the world. A Scout/Sniper Team moving carefully through an area leaving little sign of movement, will be difficult to follow for inexperienced trackers. Most people won't even notice the sign or if they do have enough training to use that sign to determine a movement of travel and follow it.

Critical Times

Certain times on any given mission will make a team particularly vulnerable to being discovered by trackers. If a team moves by night and harbors up by day, they stand a greater chance of being discovered in the afternoon, when the tracker have had sufficient time to follow the trail. If a team hides by night and only moves during the day, the team may have fast tracker walk up on the team from the rear, or may have enemy near their hide site at dusk. OP's are always vulnerable to being discovered by trackers.

Deception

Scout/Sniper Teams can take deceptive measures to confuse and slow down trackers. Deceptions are mainly done as a precautionary measure, since by the time the team knows they are being tracked; it is too late for deceptions. The guerrilla sniper will find deceptions to be useful.

The Big Tree

In this technique, the team will leave a false trail to an open area, where tracking is usually more difficult. As the team approaches a large tree, the first two people will make a 45 degree turn at the tree and head towards a nearby open area. The second pair will reach the tree and then jump straight ahead (around the tree) in the direction of travel. This is the jump spot. Naturally, where the second pair land is the landing spot. The landing spot should be clear of high vegetation which would indicate this movement, but it is useful to jump over a small bush or log to mark the landing spot. The first pair will continue to move into the open area for a short distance, after which they will carefully move backward to the jump spot. At the jump spot, the first pair will also jump to the landing spot. The team will cover their tracks here as best as possible, and will then continue on their route of travel. Any tracker following the team will hopefully waste much time in the open area, looking for further signs of the team.

Trail Backtracking

Change of direction near a marked track is used when moving through a know area and upon an established track going at right angles to your line of movement. Before reaching the track (100 meters) change direction and approach the track at a 45-degree angle. When arriving at the track continue forward along the track 20 to 30 meters, leaving considerable ground and top sign of your presence. Then walk backward to the point where you joined the track, go straight across the track and leave no sign of re-entering the vegetation. Then move off for 100 meters at an angle of 45 degrees, but this time on the other side of the track and in the reverse of your approach march. Detail the last member of the team to cover up all signs of movement. When changing direction back to the original line of travel, the Big Tree technique can be used. The purpose of this tactic is to draw a following party along the easier going jungle track. You have, by changing direction before reaching the track, indicated that this is your new line of travel. If you are successful, the following party will be casting and searching even farther away in the wrong direction when they realize that they have lost the track.

Stream Backtracking

Streams are outstanding areas in which to lay deceptions; the murkier the water, the better. The only problem with using elaborate deceptions in streams is that streams are danger areas. The figure shows a technique using multiple false exits. Notice that only one pair leaves the false track for the team. Another technique is to leave two or more false exits, and then double back on the stream itself. Imagination is the only limiting factor for laying deceptions in stream banks. In clear streams deep enough to float in, laying deceptions upstream, and then floating downstream for a good distance (using packs or poncho rafts) is an excellent deception, since the trackers will follow signs left on the stream bottom.

Ambush

If trackers are closing in on the team, the team will be forced to fight. The best technique to use is an ambush. The team must first put as much distance between themselves and the trackers as possible. If able, lure the trackers into an open area call for fire on the trackers when they enter the kill zone. The team may opt to let artillery or crew served weapons neutralize or destroy the trackers alone, or the team can use precision sniper fire also. The tracker, dog and dog handler are all primary targets. Once the ambush is complete, the team should break contact and abort the mission.

This page is intentionally left blank

About The Author

Roy A Woodall, Jr has been an active member of the military and law enforcement since 1987. He started his military career at age 17 in the United States Army Infantry. Roy deployed overseas in support of Operation Desert Storm and numerous overseas training missions as a soldier. He achieved the rank of Staff Sergeant and served as an Infantryman and Combat Engineer. In 1992 Roy started his law enforcement career as a patrol officer in a medium size city. He spent the majority of his career serving as a SWAT team sniper, firearms instructor, and weapons armorer. As a tactical officer, Roy has participated in countless critical incidents, officer involved shootings, and SWAT operations. He is a graduate of the Federal Law Enforcement Firearms Instructor Program, numerous SWAT schools, and sniper schools. Since his retirement Roy has worked overseas for the U.S. State Department as a Law Enforcement advisor serving in Iraq, Afghanistan, Nepal, Italy, and Burkina Faso. Roy has authored numerous books and magazine articles specializing in leadership, training, survival, and tactics.

night vision goggles
camo-suit
range finder
1st aid
communication
compass + maps
scope / IR ≤ 6x
Global Positioning System